REGULAR LIFE
Monastic, Canonical,
and Mendicant *Rules*

Second Edition

Documents of Practice Series

This series, published by Medieval Institute Publications at Western Michigan University in conjunction with TEAMS, is designed to offer a focused collection of primary-source materials in a classroom-friendly format. Though the topics illuminated by these booklets are generally familiar to teachers and students in various fields of medieval studies, the booklets allow readers to concentrate on a single topic or theme, either as the principal reading for a specific unit or topic within a course or as a running supplement to topics and readings being used through a semester. The topics have been chosen so they either can be seen as focal points of attention on their own, or can be used to offer a historical dimension to material used in courses on literature, women's studies, the history of medicine, religious studies, and other such areas—areas that draw a wide range of students who are being introduced to the use of primary materials and to interdisciplinary and many-layered views of the structure of medieval society and culture.

A Note From the General Editor of "Documents of Practice"

In 1997 Douglas J. McMillan and Kathryn Smith Fladenmuller prepared *Regular Life: Monastic, Canonical, and Mendicant Rules* as a booklet for the "Documents of Practice" series. The booklet has proved to be a best seller, and after two reprintings of the original version we decided that a second edition—revised and considerably expanded—would give our audience more information, more for their money. The original editors were asked if they would be interested in undertaking this work; only after they declined did we turn to Daniel La Corte, who built on the work he inherited but who has been given the freedom to make changes and alterations as he thinks best.

General Editor of the Series
Joel T. Rosenthal, *State University of New York–Stony Brook*

Advisory Editorial Board
Charlotte Newman Goldy, *Miami University of Ohio*
William Chester Jordan, *Princeton University*
Ralph V. Turner, *Florida State University (Emeritus)*

REGULAR LIFE
Monastic, Canonical,
and Mendicant *Rules*

Second Edition

Selected and Introduced by
Daniel Marcel La Corte
and
Douglas J. McMillan

Published for TEAMS
(The Consortium for the Teaching of the Middle Ages)

by

MEDIEVAL INSTITUTE PUBLICATIONS
Kalamazoo, Michigan
2004

Printed in the United States of America
P 6 5 4 3 2

Cover and design by Linda K. Judy

Composed by Julie Scrivener

ISBN 1-58044-079-7

Library of Congress Cataloging-in-Publication Data

Regular life : monastic, canonical, and mendicant rules / selected and
introduced by Daniel Marcel La Corte and Douglas J. McMillan.--
2nd ed.
    p. cm. -- (Documents of practice series)
Includes bibliographical references.
    ISBN 1-58044-079-7 (pbk. : alk. paper)
1. Monasticism and religious orders--Rules. 2. Monasticism and
religious orders--History--Early church, ca. 30-600--Sources. I. La
Corte, Daniel Marcel, 1963- II. McMillan, Douglas J., 1931- III.
Series

    BX2436.R45 2004   2003023548
    255--dc22

CONTENTS

PERMISSIONS ACKNOWLEDGMENTS

Selections from the following works were made possible by the kind permission of their respective publishers and representatives:

Quotations from St. Antony are from Athanasius, *The Life of Antony and the Letter to Marcellinus*, trans. Robert C. Gregg (New York: Paulist Press, 1980). Used by permission of Paulist Press (www.paulistpress.com). Also, we acknowledge an excerpt from *The Letters of St. Antony the Great*, trans. Derwas J. Chitty (Fairacres, Oxford: S.L.G. Press, 1975, 1977). Used by permission of the publisher.

Quotations from Pseudo-Athanasius, *The Life and Regimen of the Blessed and Holy Syncletica*, trans. Elizabeth Bryson Bongie (Toronto: Peregrina, 2001) and Waldebert, *The Rule of a Certain Father to the Virgins*, trans. Jo Ann McNamara and John Halborg, 2nd edition (Toronto: Peregrina, 1993) are used by permission of Peregrina Publishing Co.

Quotations from St. Pachomius are from *Pachomian Koinonia: The Lives, Rules and Other Writings of Saint Pachomius and His Disciples*, trans. Armand Veilleux, 3 vols. (Kalamazoo, Mich.: Cistercian Publications, 1980). Used by permission of Cistercian Publications.

Quotations from St. Basil, *The Long Rules*, are from *The Fathers of the Church: A New Translation*, trans. M. Monica Wagner, vol. 9 (Washington, D.C.: Catholic University of America Press, 1950). Used by permission of the publisher.

Quotations from John Cassian, *The Conferences*, trans. Boniface Ramsey, Ancient Christian Writers: The Works of the Fathers in Translation 57 (New York: Paulist Press, 1997) are used by permission of Paulist Press (www.paulistpress.com).

Quotations from St. Augustine, *The Rule of Our Holy Father St. Augustine: Bishop of Hippo*, trans. Robert Russell, O.S.A. (Villanova, Penn.: Province of St. Thomas of Villanova, 1976) are used by permission of the publisher.

Quotations from The Master are from *The Rule of the Master*, trans. Luke Eberle, Cistercian Studies 6 (Kalamazoo, Mich.: Cistercian Publications, 1977). Used by permission of Cistercian Publications.

Quotations from St. Benedict are from *The Rule of St. Benedict*, ed. Timothy Fry (Collegeville, Minn.: The Liturgical Press, 1982). Used by permission of the publisher.

Quotations from *Sancti Columbani Opera*, ed. G. S. M. Walker (Shannon, Ireland: Irish University Press, 1957, 1970) are used by permission of the publisher.

Quotations from Robin Bruce Lockhart, *Listening to Silence: An Anthology of Carthusian Writings* (London: Darton, Longman, & Todd, 1997) are used by permission of the publisher.

Quotations from Louis Julius Lekai, *The Cistercians: Ideals and Reality* (Kent, Ohio: Kent State University Press, 1977) are used by permission of Kent State University Press.

Quotations from J. M. Upton-Ward, trans., *The Rule of the Templars: The French Text of the Rule of the Order of the Knights Templar* (Woodbridge, Suffolk, U.K.: Boydell Press, 1992) are used by permission of Boydell Press.

Quotations from *St. Francis of Assisi: Writings and Early Biographies: English Omnibus of the Sources for the Life of St. Francis*, ed. Marion A. Habig, 4th rev. ed. (Quincy, Ill.: Quincy College-Franciscan Press, 1991) and *Rule and Testament of St. Clare: Constitutions for Poor Clare Nuns*, trans. Mary Francis (Chicago: Franciscan Herald Press) are used by permission of Franciscan Press.

Quotations from St. Dominic, found in *Saint Dominic: Biographical Documents*, ed. Francis C. Lehner (Washington, D.C.: Thomist Press, 1964), are used by permission of the publisher.

PREFACE

The phrase "regular life" refers to the lives of men and women who follow a written Rule of life. Those living under a *Regula* or Rule are generally called monastics, from the Greek word *monos*, which translates as "alone." Most often, those people following a *Regula* are lay people, not priests, who withdraw from the world to devote their lives to God, either in community or in solitude. The Rule is a way of organizing one's life with this spiritual purpose in mind. Monks, nuns, monasteries, and Rules have existed from almost the very beginning of Christianity. There are, of course, also ascetics in other religions, and ascetic Jewish sects (Nazarites and Essenes) predated and co-existed with Christianity. These Rules are interesting in themselves and indispensable for an understanding of medieval culture.

Early in Christian history, some considered the regular life as a more perfect form of the Christian life, based on Christ's own words in the Gospel of Matthew, 19:29, where Jesus says: "Anyone who has given up houses or brothers or sisters or father or mother or children, or lands for sake of my name will receive a hundred times more and inherit eternal life." Giving up these things is considered to be a renunciation of the world and also has its roots in the Christian Gospels. Matthew 14:13 tells us that Jesus "withdrew . . . into a desert place by himself." And John 6:15 says Jesus "withdrew again to the mountain by himself." A Rule helps a person to "renounce"—to put it better "reorder"—one's attachment to the material world as well as those self-centered concerns which may limit spiritual growth and total communion with God.

A life of withdrawal is fashioned on an understanding of the human condition, an anthropology. The regular life presupposes that humans are both body and soul, uniquely combined so that physical realities have an impact on a person's spiritual reality. Those seeking withdrawal believe that by changing one's environment and imposing self-discipline, one might then more properly focus on spiritual things. Additionally, in the Christian context, ascetics believe that the greatest obstacle to spiritual fulfillment is sin, which is believed to be a condition of the soul. Not a few ascetics have written that the foremost obstacle prohibiting spiritual growth is self-centeredness: pride. Fortunately this condition that affects the human will can indeed be overcome through self-discipline and grace. Therefore, regular discipline, by attempting to provide assistance to the unruly human will, fully regulates physical things for spiritual ends. For example, many Rules address issues involving clothing, food, and sleeping conditions. By limiting one's attachment to such things, a person might better focus on others and on spiritual things and one will spend less time focusing on one's self, one's appearance, and one's physical appetites. Ideally, a monk freed from mundane attachments and self-centeredness begins to be re-formed and re-educated in spiritual wisdom. However, finding the proper balance between true necessity and superfluity is also a continual concern of many monastic authorities, and thus, the need for specific guidance in the form of a Rule.

Our concern is with the Rules that governed the lives of members of medieval religious orders in the Christian tradition, particularly in western Europe. Those following a Rule during this time period can be grouped as either monastics, canons, or mendicants. Monastic orders of those nuns and monks following a Rule developed very early in the history of the Church, at least by the third century, out of the experiences of those who chose to live the life of a hermit or recluse, either alone or, later, in isolated groups. Canonical orders are generally secular priests or nuns who work in "the world." Rule-following canons and canonesses were developed much later, in the eleventh century. Mendicants are Rule-following friars, nuns, and lay persons who live out their lives in evangelical poverty, preaching, and teaching the Gospel, usually moving freely from place to place, free from a monastic enclosure and community. Mendicants developed during the late twelfth and early thirteenth centuries. All of these orders had individual Rules of life by which their members were to live.

The purpose of this book is to introduce the reader to the Rules of life of the major religious orders within the monastic, canonical, and mendicant traditions. We present the most important Rules of religious life, mainly as developed in western Europe, and we offer selections from these Rules and other documents to illustrate the ideals established for the members of the various orders through the fourteenth century. In some cases, those following a particular Rule initiate a re-form, re-evaluating their interpretation of that Rule and how best to live a life according to their Rule. In other cases the Rule might not be changed, but re-form might include a new approach to an existing Rule. We have included a textual selection, foundation documents, or other evidence which best reflects the goals of the reformers and the practical effects on the regular life. Additionally, we offer selections from these Rules and supporting documents which shed light on the spiritual aspects of the life according to a Rule.

Monasteries are experiencing increased visitors and retreatants each year, welcoming people from all walks of life and religious backgrounds to experience something of the monastic life. Regular life was a major factor in medieval and modern history, and has been the inspiration of creative writers from before Chaucer to the late twentieth century. A clue to its enduring fascination lies in this passage from the most famous and influential of the medieval Rules, that of St. Benedict: "Whoever you are, if you wish to follow the path to God, make use of this little Rule for beginners. Thus at length, you will come to the heights of doctrine and virtue under God's guidance. Amen" (St. Benedict, *Rule*, chap. 73).

INTRODUCTION

The religious Rules of life were composed to give guidance to those Christians who wished to live ascetic lives within communities of like-minded men or women. These were so-called Religious because they had chosen to live a life in accord with a Rule (*Regula*) rather than a secular life (one lived by either lay or ordained persons without such a Rule to follow). The Religious chose the ascetic way as (from their perspectives, at least) the higher way, the more perfect way, the more apostolic way, the more Christ-like way, the truly religious way to live. This approach to the Christian life developed into a life centered on prayer and work (*ora et labora*), on silence and seclusion, following Christ in poverty and obedience.

REGULAR LIFE: HISTORICAL BACKGROUND

An examination of the medieval historical development of the various Rules and orders of men and women suggests that regular life began with the lives of hermits and with early communal monastic traditions in the first six centuries of Christianity. Canonical traditions began at the same time or earlier, but seem to have been lost and were revived for religious orders only in the eleventh century. Mendicant traditions began in the twelfth and thirteenth centuries.

Monasticism (the coenobitic or common or community life) grew out of the ascetic and religious custom of living alone as a hermit, anchorite, or anchoress. These religious saw solitude as a way of saving one's soul while just barely living in the world, and certainly not being

1

of it. Of course, eremitical life continued long after monasticism itself developed and could be, on occasion, a special and higher part of monastic life. Thus the eremitical tradition (particularly among anchoresses) flourished well into the fourteenth century. The early founders of monasticism often began as hermits and then turned to the communal life and to the writing of Rules for men and women seeking salvation in community. These eremitical traditions had their origins in Egypt in the years before Constantine's imperial reign (306–37).

Those drawn to this rigorous form of life must have believed that they were called to a higher or truer form of Christianity than the one customarily followed at the time. They believed that the time of the holy martyrs had passed and that Christianity had become too comfortable. They were not only ascetic Christians in belief but also revolutionary Christians of a dedicated sort. The asceticism that started as unusual and exceptional became, within a few centuries, almost a norm— another example of how one generation's liberal becomes the next one's conservative.

These early ascetics, the so-called Desert Elders, are best represented by St. Anthony and St. Syncletica. St. Anthony the Great of Egypt (251–356), who is usually known as the first monk, was an anchorite or a godly hermit. However, he was not a "pure" hermit like St. Paul of Egypt, for he organized a community of hermits who lived in close proximity to one another, although they cherished solitude and silence. For some time Anthony led and instructed a large monastic family before he eventually retired to the desert in the area of the Red Sea. Another exemplar of the solitary life is Syncletica, who lived during the later part of the fourth century and gives witness to the spiritual life of a female desert anchorite. The *Life of Syncletica* demonstrates a deep understanding of the eremitic life and emphasizes the eremitic search for God the same as St. Anthony. The other central figure in the history of regular life is Pachomius (286–346), another hermit and monk of the East, credited with being the first hermit to establish a monastery and to write a Rule. In 315, Pachomius, following what he considered divine inspiration, became the founder of a family of monks who lived and worked together. By the time of his death he was the father of a group of monasteries with perhaps as many as 5,000 monks. Pachomius's Rule organized the details of a monastic institution, which physically consisted of a church, a refectory, an assembly room, cells, and an enclosure wall. The selected texts highlight the daily life of prayer and work in addition to the spiritual disciplines of chastity, poverty, and obedience.

From these origins monasticism spread through the eastern Mediterranean (Syria, Palestine, and Asia Minor). St. Jerome (ca. 340–420) founded a monastery in Bethlehem where monks copied both Christian and pagan manuscripts. Many other figures also date from the years before more widely used monastic Rules were formulated and disseminated. It is when monk hermits started banding together, however, that we can begin to trace the growth of communal religious (monastic) life and the beginning of the need for a Rule or Rules.

RULES FOR EASTERN ORDERS OF MONKS AND NUNS

Because monasticism originated in Egypt, its origins, like those of Christianity itself, are eastern. Indeed, even the first western monks—those in Gaul, Italy, and elsewhere—initially followed eastern Rules, especially those of Pachomius and of Basil. Monasticism flourished throughout the Byzantine Empire and the eastern Mediterranean, with special strength in Constantinople. But in the East it did not divide into different orders, as it did in the West. It is better understood as having two main forms in the eastern tradition: 1) the communal or the monastic (coenobium), and 2) the eremitical, whereby a small group of individuals (lavra, skete) lived an individual, personal life.

Perhaps more than any other figure, St. Basil (ca. 330–79) can be seen as the father and patriarch of eastern monasticism. Though his monastic writings were not offered as a structured Rule, they came to be treated as though they were a single Rule and were used and referred to by both eastern and western leaders as the Rule of St. Basil. The monasteries that sprung up to follow his lead were known as homes of charity, and they often served as orphanages, hospitals, workhouses, farms, and hospices. This still influential Rule of St. Basil (composed 358–64) exists in two forms, one of fifty-five questions and answers, the other of 313 questions and answers. This book concerns itself with the fifty-five question-and-answer form, which is known as the Long Rules of St. Basil. His words on the monastic life influenced Western ascetics like St. Benedict who two hundred years later recommended his works to his followers in the last chapter of his own rule (Chapter 73).

John Cassian (ca. 360–ca. 435), an eastern monk with experiences in Egypt and Palestine and then in Marseilles, brought eastern ideas about asceticism and the common life to the western Empire. Cassian became recommended reading throughout the history of monasticism. He succinctly summed up the core of early monasticism this way, identifying the spiritual aspects as the focus of such a life:

> Thus fasts, vigils, meditation on Scripture, and the being stripped and deprived of every possession are not perfection, but they are the tools of perfection. For the end of that discipline does not consist in these things; rather, it is by them that one arrives at the end. . . . For in following this rule we shall be able both to avoid the byways of errors and distractions and, thanks to a clear direction, to arrive at the desired end. (*Conferences*, from the "First Conference: On the goal of the Monk," Ramsey, 46).

Eastern forms of monasticism greatly influenced western monastic development in general, and Celtic (mainly Irish) monasticism was especially affected. While in the more Romanized parts of Christian Europe the urban bishoprics exerted much power and influence, in the Celtic world monasteries were the major focus of religious life and organization. Indeed, Celtic bishops usually lived in monasteries under the rule of an abbot, an eastern rather than western practice. St. Columbanus gave a Rule which made its way into Western Europe and had a terrific influence until the ninth century. In general, however (with the noted exception of Ireland and other Celtic areas), western monasticism had its own distinctly Roman-centered development, which we can now trace in more detail.

RULES FOR WESTERN ORDERS OF MONKS AND NUNS

Although the Rule of St. Benedict dominated monasticism in the West from the sixth to the eleventh centuries and beyond, there are at least two earlier important western Rules. One was that of St. Augustine of Hippo (ca. 397), although it only became influential with the development of orders of canons and canonesses/nuns in the eleventh and twelfth centuries. The other early Rule of importance was that of St. Caesarius of Arles, *The Rule for Nuns* (534), considered by many to be the prototypical western Rule of nuns.

St. Augustine (354–430), Bishop of Hippo in North Africa and one of the doctors of the church, gave the whole of western theology its defining form. His Rule of St. Augustine was famous in its own day, and was used by St. Caesarius of Arles to create his Rule for Nuns. But Augustine's Rule became most important in the eleventh century, when it became the guiding document for the newly founded orders of regular canons. Augustine's Rule, written in one form for men and in another for women, eventually served as the Rule for Augustinian, Austin, Black, or regular canons (as opposed to secular canons, who did not follow a Rule), and for regular canonesses/nuns. In the early thirteenth century it became the Rule for Dominican friars and nuns.

St. Caesarius of Arles (470–542) borrowed from the Rule of St. Augustine for about two-thirds of chapters 1–47 in his Rule for Nuns. There is strong reason to believe that Caesarius' Rule is at the core of most later Rules for nuns, including that of the Benedictine nuns. However, Ceasarius' Rule for nuns introduced a command for strict claustration which was not stressed in the Celtic Rule of Columbanus or that of St. Benedict.

The most significant establishment of a monastery and writing of a Rule in western Christendom is ascribed to St. Benedict of Nursia (480–547), whose justifiably famous and tremendously influential Rule for Monks was written about 535–45. It is Benedict's Rule which dominates western monasticism throughout its growth and series of reforms; what monasticism was, and is, in the West is essentially what St. Benedict portrayed in his Rule. Benedict studied at Rome, became a hermit, gathered disciples around himself, founded twelve monasteries of twelve monks each with abbots of whom he approved, and prepared his Rule for his own monastery of Monte Cassino, about halfway between Naples and Rome. His sister and disciple, St. Scholastica, established a hermitage for women near Monte Cassino, and she has been patron saint of all Benedictine women's communities ever since.

Benedict drew from the Rule of St. Basil and the Rule of St. Augustine; however, his main source was the *Regula Magistri*, the "Rule of the Master." Benedict selected whole sections from the *Regula Magistri* and followed "the Master" to a large extent. Despite this, his Rule is original in its brevity, clarity, and universality. The numerous reforms of monasticism that came periodically through the Middle Ages were basically reinterpretations of Benedict's Rule. Some of the reinterpretations were fairly drastic. The general nature of Benedict's Rule means that it lends itself to wide variation of interpretation and implementation. Furthermore, the regular routines of canons, members of religious military orders, and members of mendicant orders were also variations on and reactions to Benedict's Rule and his vision of the regular life.

Although eastern monasticism continued to emphasize its eremitical roots, Western monasticism developed rapidly along coenobitic lines and forms. Western monasteries were meant to be self-sufficient agricultural establishments and many flourished and enjoyed great success. Monks became excellent farmers and developed agricultural techniques and devices of long-lasting significance. In part as a consequence of their spiritual leadership and asceticism, many houses received donations—some in the form of land—and in this way their very success bred trouble. By the sixteenth century in England, the power of the secular lords led them to desire to retake the huge aggregations of monastic lands and wealth. During the English Reformation, monastic lands and buildings were confiscated by the secular authorities, and within a few years a significant portion of the realm's wealth, which had been in monastic hands, was quickly redistributed, mostly for political reasons.

REFORMED ORDERS OF MONKS AND NUNS

In the Merovingian period (448 to 751) St. Benedict's Rule was one among many Rules for monastic life. In addition to the Rules mentioned above, St. Columbanus' Rule seemed especially popular, and was used to found Luxeuil, France, a monastery established by Irish monks. For many years elements of both Benedict's and Columbanus' Rules were combined to form the so-called "mixed rules," which essentially took features from both Rules and were adapted to suit a particular circumstance. Additionally, there were also "double monasteries" which included separate communities of men and women living in proximity, using a common church for the liturgical offices and directed by either an abbot or an abbess. However, St. Waldebert, seventh century Abbot of Luxeuil, wrote a Rule specifically for women monastics, thus illustrating the great variety of monastic options that existed during this time period.

Some effort to impose a more certain degree of uniformity upon monastic life throughout the western Church (beyond following the same Rule with varying interpretations) came in the ninth century, at the time of Charlemagne (d. 814) and his son Louis the Pious (d. 840). Benedict of Aniane, a close advisor to Charlemagne, assisted in crafting a decree to insure that all monks and nuns would follow the Rule of St. Benedict. Charlemagne died before this could be implemented, but Louis the Pious carried out the plan. Though different Benedictine monasteries were not linked as an order in a constitutional or governmental fashion, the uniformity of practice imposed by Charlemagne's decree did much to help develop a standardized approach to education, the liturgy, and regular life. The differences that resulted from the rise of the reform in subsequent centuries had more to do with the rigor of obedience than with the basic interpretation of the Rule.

By the tenth and eleventh centuries many monasteries had become too deeply involved in worldly matters, as critics inside monasticism as well as outside frequently pointed out. Through their extensive land acquisition, their operation of schools, their supplying of knights for armies, and their work with secular authorities in affairs of state, they seemed to stray from their original intentions. A series of internal reforms ensued, leading to the birth of a number of reformed orders and sub-orders that we can think of as new variations of the original Benedictine order. In fact, the reformers usually believed that they followed the Rule more strictly than the traditional Benedictines. Again, we have the important matter of different interpretations of the text of the Rule. Reforms within the Benedictine tradition included the Cluniac reform and order begun in 909.

The Cluniac reform freed its monks from both secular and episcopal interference, essentially breaking feudal bonds which had become problematic in some monasteries. Cluny's founder, William of Aquitaine, allowed abbatial elections free from the secular interference which had become customary in many parts of the west. Monks of the house at Cluny (near Lyons) followed the modifications and interpretations of the Rule of St. Benedict as they had been formulated by Benedict of Aniane (750–821). Cluny emphasized the liturgical life outlined in the Rule, which gave birth to an elaborate sequence of daily prayer and liturgical services in addition to adhering to a strict, ascetical life. Cluny dominated monastic life for well over a century. As with any successful order, critics saw its expansion and popularity as laxity and became critical of the way in which Cluny lived the monastic life.

THE CALL OF THE DESERT IN THE HIGH MIDDLE AGES: PRIMITIVE MONASTIC MODELS

The late eleventh and early twelfth centuries witnessed a reforming spirit as a reaction to the Gregorian reforms. Monastic movements looked to their primitive roots in the Desert as models for reform. Several orders were founded out of this desire to live more literally the eremitical and cenobitical lives of the Desert elders. Each order's differences can be seen in the emphasis they gave to either aspect of the Desert models.

The Cistercian reform began at Cîteaux, in Burgundy, France, in 1098. Imbued with a reforming spirit which looked to the early desert elders as their model of reform, the Cistercians interpreted the Rule more literally, emphasizing poverty, manual labor, and seclusion from the world. In order to live this more rigorous approach to the Rule, the Cistercians insisted on simplicity in all things. Their insistence on manual labor to provide for their maintenance helped them live simply by necessity, thereby limiting superfluity in all aspects of monastic life. Here we have a strict, literal interpretation of St. Benedict's Rule which helped make the Cistercians the greatest monastic force of the twelfth century.

Other similar reform orders included the Carthusians, who, while adhering to much of the Rule of Benedict in their daily life, emphasized the eremitical aspect of the Rule and provided more time in solitude. The spiritual renewal motivated two similar foundations: the Gilbertines in England and the abbey of Fontevrault in France. These orders were both double communities whose founders wanted to provide specifically for women contemplatives. In addition to various reforms within the Benedictine system, we can note the development in the early twelfth century of military orders. These men vowed to follow the Rule and, as their main purpose, to be soldiers in wars against the infidel and to protect and defend the pilgrimage routes and later provide defense of the Holy Places. The Order of the Temple, or Knights Templar, wore a red cross, took vows of chastity and obedience, lived a communal life, and assisted at the Divine Office when it was sung by canons regular. *The Rule of the Temple* was composed by St. Bernard of Clairvaux, the most famous and influential of the Cistercians, who based it on the Rule of St. Benedict and on Cistercian practices. Along with the Templars is the Order of Hospitallers, who originally began as a fraternity serving sick and poor pilgrims in the Holy Lands, but later developed into a military order by Raymond du Puy. They wore a white cross and followed the Rule of St. Augustine.

RULES FOR ORDERS OF CANONS AND CANONESSES/NUNS

The tenth through twelfth centuries saw not only reformed monastic orders—essentially Benedictine though varying considerably in degrees of strict adherence to the Rule—but also economic and social changes in western society. The development of wealthy urban centers made the monastic life either seemingly or actually out of step or out of balance with the changing current of social and economic life. Anchoritism (the life of a hermit) also returned, perhaps in reaction to the increased wealth now found in urban societies. This economic upturn of society was probably at least partially responsible also for the development of orders of canons and canonesses/nuns.

The establishment of regular canons and canonesses/nuns had its focus in cathedrals and in large cities. The canonical life was thought of as a compromise, halfway between that of the secular clergy and that of Benedictine monks. The main early canonical orders were the Norbertines or Premonstratensians, the Victorines, and the Augustinian canons and canonesses/nuns. Part of the need for these developments may have been the practice of having mainly married secular canons on cathedral staffs. Bishops would have much more control over celibate, Rule-following canons. Regular canons could be distinguished from monks because they lived by the newly revived Rule of St. Augustine, not St. Benedict.

The canonical movement drew on sources dating from a time before Benedictine monasticism became organized in the sixth century: back to St. Augustine and even further back to the Bible. Regular canons considered St. Augustine's Rule to be more biblical and apostolic than the later Rules. Augustine essentially called for having common possessions, common times of communal prayer, no individual distinctive clothing, and strict obedience to the leader of the community.

Pope Urban II (1088–99) distinguished between the monastic and the canonical forms of religious life by holding that those who followed monastic tradition gave up all earthly things for a life of contemplation, whereas those who followed canonical tradition made proper use of earthly things and did deeds both for the reparation of the sins of the world and to help the poor, sick, and infirm. The canons' numbers were indeed smaller than monastics, but the canonical tradition was of great importance nevertheless.

RULES FOR ORDERS OF FRIARS, NUNS, AND LAY PERSONS

Whereas the monks were essentially part of agricultural, rural society, and the canons worked in towns and on their fringes, the mendicant (begging) orders of friars such as the Franciscans and the Dominicans were established in further response to new social conditions. And very clearly, the friars were organized to deal with an ever-growing urban society, with its educational opportunities and its oppressive poverty for some members. The mendicants' work was clearly in the world, particularly in poor sections of towns. Both personal and corporate poverty were the initial ideal for the friars.

The mendicant orders were mainly established in the late twelfth and early thirteenth centuries. Here we have the Order of Friars Preachers (Dominicans), who followed the Rule of St. Augustine, and the Order of Friars Minor (Franciscans), who followed the newly written Rule of St. Francis. Although all these orders had divisions for men and women, the most interesting women and perhaps the most influential were the Franciscan sisters called the Poor Clares. The women of this order were totally enclosed (cloistered) and focused not on work with the world, but interior spiritual growth through poverty and prayer. Clare's insistence on poverty and simplicity is characteristic of the Poor Clares' spirituality.

St. Francis of Assisi (1181/2–1226) founded the Order of Friars Minor (the first Franciscan order) and wrote its Rule. St. Clare (1194–1253), inspired by her friend Francis, founded the Order of Poor Clares (the second Franciscan order) and wrote its Rule. Francis also founded and wrote a Rule for an order of lay men and women (the third Franciscan order). The Dominicans and other early mendicant orders, including some canonical ones, also had third orders of lay persons, and the relevant part of Francis's Rule appears below. Members of third orders could be married, live at home, and follow secular occupations, though the "third rule" allowed them to combine secular with regular life.

The nuns who chose to be members of these new orders, however, lived cloistered lives just as their monastic and canonical sisters did. Women's roles did not change as men's roles did through the course of religious and institutional development, from monasticism through canonical orders to mendicant orders. What attracted individual women to one type of order or another was the goal of the particular order, which the women supported through their membership and prayers. It was only in the later Middle Ages, with a new emphasis on lay piety and "popular religion," that women (in such groups as the Beguines) found ways of yoking the goals of a common religious life and service within the community.

The Dominican order developed out of the Augustinian canon model. However, its emphasis was on missionary work and on preaching. Its founder, St. Dominic (1170–1221), chose the Rule of St. Augustine for his Order of Friars Preachers—although his order was influenced also by the development of the Franciscan order and its unique Rule. Our selection for the Dominican Rule comes from an early biography of the order's founder and its evolution provides an ideal glimpse at the foundations of that influential order.

CONCLUSIONS

All the orders we have referred to had their various histories with high and low points. Sometimes the Rules were followed to the letter, but at other times they were nearly ignored. Reform after reform brought members of the orders back to their Rules; periods of laxity and reform occurred in cycles. Yet most orders and their Rules continue to exist and to be influential in our own day. What guided, directed, motivated, and inspired those men and women who chose to follow monastic, canonical, or mendicant lives according to the Rules of people like Basil, Augustine, Caesarius, Benedict, Francis, and Clare, might be best discovered through a close reading of the Rules themselves.

THE RULES

THE LIFE OF ANTONY

From Athanasius, *The Life of Antony and the Letter to Marcellinus*, translation and introduction by Robert C. Gregg; pp. 35–37, 41–43, 45–46, and 65. Mahwah, N. J.: Paulist Press, 1980.

Athanasius (296–373), Bishop of Alexandria; Confessor and Doctor of the Church, established the prototype for the genre of saints' Lives with his account of Saint Antony (251–356). Written about 357, shortly after Antony's death, Athanasius wrote this short Life while exiled from his episcopal seat for a third time. The Life of Antony highlights the ascetical practices of this early hermit's life—practices which became central to the lives of those who sought to remove themselves from mainstream society and its priorities on things temporal. Athanasius emphasizes silence, self-discipline in diet and performing manual labor, and meditative reading of Scripture. As a result, Antony demonstrated a sense of balance after practicing regular discipline for years. His attitude towards renunciation of the world also inspired succeeding generations of monastics as most certainly will the transformation through grace as a most important aspect of the spiritual life.

7. This was Antony's first contest against the devil—or, rather this was in Antony the success of the Savior, who "condemned sin in the flesh,

13

in order that the just requirement of the Law might be fulfilled in us, who walk not according to the flesh but according to the Spirit" (Rom. 8:3–4). From the Scriptures Antony learned that the treacheries of the enemy are numerous, and he practiced the discipline [the monastic discipline of self-denial] with intensity, realizing that although his foe had not been powerful enough to beguile him with bodily pleasure, he would surely attempt to entrap him by some other method, for the demon is a lover of sin. More and more then he mortified the body and kept it under subjection (cf. 1 Cor. 9:27) so that he would not, after conquering some challenges, trip up in others. So he made plans to accustom himself to more stringent practices, and many marveled, but he bore the labor with ease. For the eagerness that resided so long in his soul produced a good disposition in him, so that when he received from others even a small suggestion, he showed great enthusiasm for it. His watchfulness was such that he often passed the entire night without sleep, and doing this not once, but often, he inspired wonder. He ate once daily, after sunset, but there were times when he received food [only] every second and frequently even every fourth day. His food was bread and salt, and for drinking he took only water. There is no reason even to speak of meat and wine, when indeed such a thing was not found among the other zealous men. A rush mat was sufficient to him for sleeping, but more regularly he lay on the bare ground. He disapproved of oil for anointing the skin, saying that it was more fitting for youths to hold to the ascetic life intensely, and not to seek the things that relax the body, but to habituate it to labors, thinking of the Apostle's remark, "When I am weak, then I am strong" (2 Cor. 12:10). For he said the soul's intensity is strong when the pleasures of the body are weakened. And this tenet of his was also truly wonderful, that neither the way of virtue nor separation from the world for its sake ought to be measured in terms of time spent, but by the aspirant's desire and purposefulness. He, indeed, did not hold time passed in his memory, but day by day, as if making a beginning of his asceticism, increased his exertion for advance, saying continually to himself Paul's word about "forgetting what lies behind and straining forward to what lies ahead" (Phil. 3:13), and recalling also the passage in which Elijah the prophet says, "the Lord . . . lives, before whom I stand today" (1 Kings 18:15). He observed that in saying today he was not counting the time passed, but he endeavored each day to present himself as the sort of person ready to appear before God—that is, pure of heart and prepared to obey his will, and no other. And he used to tell himself that from the career of the great Elijah, as from a mirror, the ascetic must always acquire knowledge of his own life.

14. Nearly twenty years he spent in this manner pursuing the ascetic life by himself, not venturing out and only occasionally being seen by anyone. After this, when many possessed the desire and will to emulate his asceticism, and some of his friends came and tore down and forcefully removed the fortress door, Antony came forth as though from some shrine, having been led into divine mysteries and inspired by God. This was the first time he appeared from the fortress for those who came out to him. And when they beheld him, they were amazed to see that his body had maintained its former condition, neither fat from lack of exercise, nor emaciated from fasting and combat with demons, but was just as they had known him prior to his withdrawal. The state of his soul was one of purity, for it was not constricted by grief, nor relaxed by pleasure, nor affected by either laughter or dejection. Moreover, when he saw the crowd, he was not annoyed any more than he was elated at being embraced by so many people. He maintained utter equilibrium, like one guided, by reason and steadfast in that which accords with nature. Through him the Lord healed many of those present who suffered from bodily ailments; others he purged of demons, and to Antony he gave grace in speech. Thus he consoled many who mourned, and others hostile to each other he reconciled in friendship, urging everyone to prefer nothing in the world above the love of Christ. And when he spoke and urged them to keep in mind the future goods and the affection in which we are held by God, "who did not spare his own Son, but gave him up for us all" (Rom. 8:32), he persuaded so many to take up the solitary life. And so, from then on, there were monasteries in the mountains and the desert was made a city by monks, who left their own people and registered themselves for the citizenship in the heavens.

17. "Therefore, my children, let us not lose heart. Let us not think that the time is too long or what we do is great, 'for the sufferings of this present time are not worth comparing with the glory that is to be revealed to us'" (Rom. 8:18). And let us not consider, when we look at the world, that we have given up things of some greatness, for even the entire earth is itself quite small in relation to all of heaven. If now it happened that we were lords of all the earth, and renounced all the earth, that would amount to nothing as compared with the kingdom of heaven. For just as if someone might despise one copper drachma in order to gain a hundred gold drachmas, so he who is ruler of the whole earth, and renounces it, loses little, and he receives a hundred times more. But if all the earth is not equal in value to the heavens, then he who has given up a few *arourae* sacrifices virtually nothing, and even if he should give up a house or considerable wealth, he has no reason to boast or grow careless. We ought also to realize that if we do not surrender these things through virtue, then later when we die we shall leave these things behind—often, to those whom we do not wish, as Ecclesiastes reminds us (Eccles. 4:8, 6:2). This being the case, why should we not give them up for virtue's sake, so that we might inherit even a kingdom? Let none among us have even the yearning to possess. For what benefit is there in possessing these things that we do not take with us? Why not rather own those things that we are able to take away with us—such things as prudence, justice, temperance, courage, understanding, love, concern for the poor, faith in Christ, freedom from anger, hospitality? If we possess these, we shall discover them running before, preparing hospitality for us there in the land of the meek.

19. "Therefore, my children, let us hold to the discipline, and not be careless. For we have the Lord for our co-worker in this, as it is written, God 'works for good with' (cf. Rom. 8:28) everyone who chooses the good. And in order that we not become negligent, it is good to carefully consider the Apostle's statement: 'I die daily' (cf. 1 Cor. 15:42). For if we so live as people dying daily, we will not commit sin. The point of the saying is this: As we rise daily, let us suppose that we shall not survive till evening, and again, as we prepare for sleep, let us consider that we shall not awaken. By its very nature our life is uncertain,

and is meted out daily by providence. If we think this way, and in this way live—daily—we will not sin, nor will we crave anything, nor bear a grudge against anyone, nor will we lay up treasures on earth, but as people who anticipate dying each day we shall be free of possessions, we shall forgive all things to all people. The desire for a woman, or another sordid pleasure, we shall not merely control—rather, we shall turn from it as something transitory, forever doing battle and looking toward the day of judgment. For the larger fear and dread of the torments always destroys pleasure's smooth allure, and rouses the declining soul.

45. Then Antony, withdrawing by himself, as was his custom, to his own cell, intensified his discipline and sighed daily, reflecting on the dwellings in heaven, both longing for these and contemplating the ephemeral life of human beings. For also when he was about to eat or sleep or to attend to the other bodily necessities, he was ashamed as he thought about the intellectual part of the soul. Frequently when he was about to have a meal in the company of many other monks, recalling the spiritual food, he would excuse himself and go some distance from them, thinking he would blush if he were seen eating by others. He ate by himself, of course, according to his body's need, yet often with the brothers as well, doing this out of respect for them and becoming bold in the words he spoke for their assistance. He used to say that we ought to devote all our time to the soul instead of the body. He urged us to concede a little time to the body, out of necessity, but to be intent, for the most part, on the soul and to seek its benefit, so that it would not be dragged down by bodily pleasures, but rather that the body might be subservient to the soul. For this is what was said by the Savior: "Do not be anxious for your life, what you shall eat, nor about your body, what you shall put on. . . . And do not seek what you are to eat and what you are to drink, nor be of anxious mind. For all the nations of the world seek these things; and your Father knows that you need them. Instead, seek his Kingdom, and these things shall be yours as well" (Matt. 4:31; Luke 12:29).

THE LETTERS OF ST. ANTONY THE GREAT

From *The Letters of St. Antony the Great*, translated by Derwas J. Chitty, pp. 1–3. Fairacres, Oxford: S.L.G. Press, 1975; reprinted 1977.

Saint Antony (251–356) is often considered the father of monasticism, founding several colonies for hermits in the Egyptian desert towards the end of the third century. The following selection comes from St. Antony's letters to his fellows in the solitary life written around 338, not long after his well documented and rare visit to Alexandria. We have here Antony's own understanding of the various approaches to the religious life. Antony emphasizes the idea of progression and reformation of the whole person living the ascetical life. Both body and soul receive attention in this life and thus reap spiritual benefits.

A Letter of Antony the Solitary and Chief of Solitaries to the brethren dwelling in every place:

First of all—peace to your love in the Lord! I think, brethren, that the souls which draw near to the love of God are of three sorts, be they male or female.

There are those who are called by the law of love which is in their nature, and which original good implanted in them at their first creation. The word of God came to them, and they doubted not at all but followed it readily, like Abraham the Patriarch: for when God saw that it was not from the teaching of men that he had learnt to love God, but from the law implanted in the nature of his first compacting, God appeared to him and said, "Get thee out from thy country and from thy kindred and from thy father's house, unto a land that I will show thee" (Gen. 12:1). And he went nothing doubting, but was ready for his calling. He is the pattern of this approach, which still persists in those who follow in his footsteps. Toiling and seeking the fear of God in patience and quiet, they achieve the true manner of life, because their souls are ready to follow the love of God. This is the first kind of calling.

The second calling is this. There are men who hear the written Law testifying of pains and torments prepared for the wicked, and of the promises prepared for those who walk worthily in the fear of God; and by the testimony of the written Law their thoughts are roused up to seek to enter into the calling, as David testifies when he says: "The law of the Lord is undefiled, converting the soul: the testimony of the Lord is sure, and giveth wisdom unto the simple" (Ps. 19:7). And in another place he says, "The opening of thy words giveth light and understanding unto the simple" (Ps. 119:130); and much else, all of which we cannot mention now.

The third calling is this. There are souls which at first were hard of heart and persisted in the works of sin; and somehow the good God in his mercy sends upon such souls the chastisement of affliction, till they grow weary, and come to their senses, and are converted, and draw near, and enter into knowledge, and repent with all their heart, and they also attain the true manner of life, like those others of whom we have already spoken. These are the three approaches by which souls come to repentance, till they attain to the grace and calling of the Son of God.

Now, as regards those who have entered with all their heart, and have made themselves despise all afflictions of the flesh, valiantly resisting all the warfare that rises against them, until they conquer—I think that first of all, the Spirit calls them, and makes the warfare light for them, and sweetens for them the works of repentance, showing them how they ought to repent in body and soul, until He has taught them how to be converted to God who created them. And He delivers to them works whereby they may constrain their soul and their body, that both may be purified and enter together into their inheritance.

First the body is purified by much fasting, by many vigils and prayers, and by the service which makes a man to be straightened in body, cutting off from himself all the lusts of the flesh. And the Spirit of Repentance is made his guide in these things, and tests him by means of them, lest the enemy should turn him back again.

Then the Spirit that is his guide begins to open the eyes of his soul, to give to it also repentance, that it may be purified. The mind also starts to discriminate between the body and the soul, as it begins to learn from the Spirit how to purify both by repentance. And, taught by the Spirit, the mind becomes our guide to the labors of body and soul, showing us how to purify them. And it separates us from all the fruits of the flesh which have been mingled with all the members of the body since the first transgression, and brings back each of the members of the body to its original condition, having nothing in it from the spirit of Satan. And the body is brought under the authority of the mind, being taught by the Spirit, as St. Paul says: "I keep under my body, and bring it into subjection" (1 Cor. 9:17). For the mind purifies it from food and from drink and from sleep, and in a word from all its motions, until through its own purity it frees the body even from the natural emission of seed.

And, as I think, there are three types of motion of the body. There is that which is implanted in the body by nature, compacted with it in its first creation; but this is not operative if the soul does not will it, save only that it signifies its presence through a passionless movement in the body. And there is another motion, when a man stuffs his body with food and drink, and the heat of the blood from the abundance of nourishment rouses up warfare in the body, because of our greed. For this cause the Apostle said, "Be not drunk with wine, wherein is excess" (Eph. 5:18). And again the Lord enjoined His disciples, "Take heed lest at any time your hearts be overcharged with surfeiting and drunkenness" (Luke 21:34) or pleasure. Especially those who seek the measure of purity ought to be saying, "I keep under my body, and bring it into subjection" (1 Cor. 9:27). And there is a third motion, from the evil spirits which tempt us out of envy, and seek to defile those who are setting out on the way of purity.

And now, my beloved children, in these three types of motion, if the soul exerts itself and perseveres in the testimony which the Spirit bears within the mind, both soul and body are purified from this kind of sickness. But if in regard to these three motions the mind spurns the testimony which the Spirit bears within it, evil spirits take authority over it, and sow in the body all the passions, and stir up and quicken strong war against it; till the soul grows weary and sick, and cries out and seeks from whence help may come to it, and repents, and obeys the commandments of the Spirit, and is healed. Then it is persuaded to make its rest in God, and that He is its peace.

These things I have said to you, beloved, that you may know how it is required of a man to repent in body and soul, and to purify them both. And if the mind conquers in this contest, then it prays in the Spirit, and begins to expel from the body the passions of the soul which come to it from its own will. Then the Spirit has a loving partnership with the mind, because the mind keeps the commandments which the Spirit has delivered to it. And the Spirit teaches the mind how to heal all the wounds of the soul, and to rid itself of every one, those which are mingled in the members of the body, and other passions which are altogether outside the body, being mingled in the will. And for the eyes it sets a rule, that they may see rightly and purely, and that in them there may be no guile. After that it sets a rule also for the ears, how they may hear in peace, and no more thirst or desire to hear ill speaking, nor about the falls and humiliations of men; but how they may rejoice to hear about good things, and about the way every man stands firm and about the mercy shown to the whole creation, which in these members once was sick.

THE LIFE AND REGIMEN OF THE BLESSED
AND HOLY SYNCLETICA

From Pseudo-Athanasius, *The Life and Regimen of the Blessed and Holy Syncletica*, translated with notes by Elizabeth Bryson Bongie. Peregrina Translations Series no. 21. Toronto: Peregrina Publishing Co., 1999; reprinted, with corrections, 1996, 1997, 1998.

The Life of Syncletica was written shortly after Syncletica's death in the early part of the fifth century. It is believed that Syncletica lived in the last part of the fourth century, born into a well-known Christian family from Macedonia living in the seaport of Alexandria. Syncletica was one of several women who lived the eremitical life when solitaries were beginning to live in small communities. Excerpts of Syncletica's Life were included in the famous *The Sayings of the Desert Fathers*, a collection of spiritual wisdom which contains very few women's voices. This *Life of Syncletica* emphasizes an insistence on worldly renunciation and interior growth which places her solidly in the tradition of the desert hermits. Humility and love are central themes guiding the reform and perfection of the monastic.

12. "After distributing all her substance to the poor, she said: 'I have been judged worthy of a great title. What worthy return shall I make to the giver? I do not have anything. If in the outside world, for the sake of a transitory distinction, people throw away their whole substance, how much more necessary is it for me who have been granted so great a grace to offer my body along with what are regarded as possessions? But why do I talk about giving possessions or body when all that is belongs to him? For the Lord's is the earth and its fullness' (Ps. 24:1). Once she had 'clothed herself with humility' (cf. 1 Pet. 5:5) by means of these words, she entered upon a solitary life.

13. "Even in her father's house, however, she was reasonably well practiced in austerities and was already making progress in virtue when she

entered upon this crucial stage of her course. Those people, you see, who come to this divine mystery without training and reflection do not find what they seek, since they have not first examined what is needed in detail. But just as those contemplating a journey first think about their provisions, so she also prepared herself over time with austerities and generously provided herself with the necessities for her journey to the heights. For, by arranging in advance what she needed for the construction of her building, she succeeded in making her tower very sturdy (cf. Luke 14:28). Now the construction of buildings is traditionally carried out with materials from without, but she went about it in the opposite way; she did not gather all her building materials from without, but rather she emptied herself of what was within. For by giving her possessions to the poor, by relinquishing anger and vindictiveness, and by driving away envy and ambition, she built her house on rock, its tower visible from afar and its structure storm proof (cf. Matt. 7:24).

14. "And why do I go on at length? In her beginnings she surpassed even those who were accustomed to the solitary life. Just as the most naturally gifted children, while still learning their letters, compete with those who are older and have spent more time with their teachers, so also this woman, fervent in spirit, sprinted past all other women.

15. "We cannot speak, then, of her actual ascetic life, since she did not allow anyone to be an observer of this. Nor did she wish her associates to be 'heralds' of her heroic virtues. For she did not so much think about doing good as she did about keeping her good works private and secret. She acted in this way not because she was pressured by envy, but because she was supported by divine grace. For she kept in mind that saying of the Lord to the effect: 'if your right hand does something, let your left hand not know it' (cf. Matt. 6:3). And thus, in private, she fulfilled the demands of her calling."

20. "Her life, therefore, was apostolic, constrained by faith and holy poverty, yet still, to be sure, radiant with love and humility. Her conduct was the fulfillment of the saving word. 'For you shall tread upon

asp and viper' (cf. Ps. 91:13) and 'on all the power of the enemy' (Luke 10:19). Fittingly she heard this message: 'Well done, good and faithful servant; you were faithful in a few matters, I shall set you up over many' (cf. Matt. 25:21). Even though this message refers to gifts, in this instance nevertheless it should be interpreted in the following way: 'Because you were victorious in the war of the flesh, you will also carry off a trophy in the war of the spirit, under the protection of my shield. Let those principalities and powers spoken of by my servant Paul know the greatness of your faith; for, since you have vanquished the opposing forces, you will encounter even stronger ones.' Thus, then, going apart on her own, she continued perfecting her good works. And as time progressed and her virtues were blossoming, the sweet scent (2 Cor. 2:15) of her widely renowned austerities spread to many, for, Scripture says, 'Nothing is hidden which will not be revealed' (cf. Matt. 10:26). Even on his own God knows how to proclaim those who love him for the correction of those who listen. At that time, therefore, some women began to come by in their wish for something better and to make appeals for their edification. Since, in fact, they profited through their discussions in exchanging information about Syncletica's life, they began to come more and more often in their desire to be helped. According to their customary procedure they would put questions to her, saying: 'How must one be saved?' And with a deep groan and a flood of tears, she would withdraw into herself and would again observe silence as if her tears were answer enough. But the women, acting as a group, would force her to speak of the great deeds of God. Actually they were stunned and amazed just by the sight of her. Again they would call upon her to speak. And under great pressure, after quite a long time spent in deepest silence, the blessed woman would recite in a low voice that passage from Scripture: 'Do no violence to a poor man, for he is needy' (Prov. 22:22). The women present received this response gladly as if they had tasted of honey and honeycomb, and continued their questioning even more. And from then on they used to challenge her through scriptural passages, for they would say to her: 'You received a gift, give a gift' (cf. Matt. 10:8). Or they might say: 'See to it that you do not pay instead of the servant for the hidden talent' (cf. Matt. 25:30). But she would say to them: 'Why do you fantasize in this way about a sinner like me as if I were doing or saying something worthwhile? We have a common teacher—the Lord; we draw spiritual water from the same well and we suck our milk from the same breasts—the Old and the New Testaments.' But they would say to her: 'We also know that we have one source of instruction—Scripture—and the same teacher. But you have made progress in virtues by your ever-wakeful zeal; those who are in possession of what is good, since they are better able, must also help those who are weaker. And indeed our common teacher commands this.' And on hearing these words, the blessed woman used to weep, like a babe at the breast. But the women gathered there put aside their questioning once more and urged her to stop weeping. And when she had grown calm, there was again a long period of silence and again they began to encourage her. Since she was deeply moved and knew, moreover, that what she had said did not bring praise for herself but rather sowed helpful ideas among those present, she began to speak to them in the following vein."

22. "My children, all of us—male and female—know about being saved, but through our own negligence we stray from the path of salvation. First of all we must observe the precepts known through the grace of the Lord, and these are: 'You shall love the Lord your God with your whole soul, and your neighbor as yourself' (cf. Matt. 22:37, 39). In these precepts the first principle of the Law is preserved, and it is on this Law that the fullness of grace depends. The expression of the principle is brief indeed, but its importance in this matter is great and unlimited, for all advice to help the soul depends on these precepts. Paul also bears witness to this when he says that the 'end of law is love' (cf. Rom. 13:10; 1 Tim. 1:5). Whatever people say by the grace of the Spirit, therefore, that is useful springs from love and ends in it. Salvation, then, is exactly this—the two-fold love of God and of our neighbor."

42. "Let us women not be misled by the thought that those in the world are without cares. For perhaps in comparison they struggle more than we do. For towards women generally there is great hostility in the world. They bear children with difficulty and risk, and they suffer patiently through nursing, and they share illnesses with their sick children—and these things they endure without having any limit to their

travail. For either the children they bear are maimed in body, or, brought up in perversity, they treacherously murder their parents. Since we women know these facts, therefore, let us not be deluded by the Enemy that their life is easy and carefree. For in giving birth women die in labor; and yet, in failing to give birth, they waste away under reproaches that they are barren and unfruitful.

43. "I am telling you these things to safeguard you from the Adversary. What is being said, however, is not suitable for all, but only for those who choose the monastic life. For just as one diet is not suitable for all animals, so the same instruction is not appropriate for all people. As Scripture says: 'one should not put new wine into old wineskins' (Matt. 9:17). Those who find satisfaction in contemplation and spiritual enlightenment [*gnosis*] are nourished in one way, while those who have a taste for asceticism and its practical application [*praktike*] are nourished in another way, and similarly those in the world who practice good works to the best of their ability. For just as some living creatures are land animals, some are water animals, and some winged, so also are human beings; some people choose the middle road (as land animals do), some look to the heights (as birds do), and others (like fish) are concealed in the waters of their sins. Scripture says: 'I came into the depths of the sea, and a storm engulfed me' (Ps. 69:2). And such is the nature of living creatures. But since we women have grown wings like eagles, let us soar to the higher places, and let us trample underfoot the lion and the dragon (cf. Ps. 90:13); and let us now rule over the one who once ruled over us. And this we shall do if we offer to the Savior our whole mind."

93. "Just as it is not possible to bring up at the same time two buckets filled with water since, by the turning of the windlass, the one bucket is lowered empty and the other is brought up full, so it is in our case. When we apply to the soul total concern, it is brought up filled with virtues and pointed towards heaven. And our body (which has become light through discipline) does not weigh down the leading force [of the counterbalance]. And of this the Apostle is witness for he says: 'Inasmuch as our outer person is destroyed, so much is the inner person renewed' (cf. 2 Cor. 4:16).

94. "Do you live in a cenobitic monastery? Do not change your location, for you will be greatly harmed. For just as a bird that abandons its eggs renders them empty and unfruitful, so a nun or a monk grows cold and dies to faith by moving from place to place.

95. "Let not the delights of those who are wealthy by worldly standards entice you as being something useful. For the sake of pleasure they honor the culinary art; by fasting and through frugality surpass their superabundance of foodstuffs. For Scripture says: 'A soul, when satisfied, scorns honey' (Prov. 27:7). Do not fill up with bread and you will not crave wine.

96. "The main sources of the Enemy from which every evil springs are threefold: desire, pleasure, sadness. These are connected one from another, and one follows another. It is possible to control pleasure to some extent, but impossible to control desire; for the end of pleasure is achieved through the body, but that [of desire] originates from the soul, while sadness is concocted from both. Well then, do not allow desire to become active, and you will dissipate the remaining two. But if you permit the first to emerge, it will develop into the second and they will form with one another 'a vicious circle'; and in no way will the soul be allowed to escape. For Scripture says: 'Do not grant a way out to water' (Sir. 25:25 [Ecclus. 25:15]).

97. "Not all courses are suitable for all people. Each person should have confidence in his own disposition, because for many it is profitable to live in a community. And over others it is helpful to withdraw on their own. For just as some plants become more flourishing when they are in humid locations, while others are more stable in drier conditions, so also among humans, some flourish in the higher places, while others achieve salvation in the lower places. Many people, then, have found salvation in a city, while imagining the conditions of a desert. And many, though on a mountain, have been lost by living the life of townspeople. It is possible for one who is in a group to be alone in thought, and for one who is alone to live mentally with a crowd."

PACHOMIAN KOINONIA I: THE FIRST SAHIDIC LIFE OF PACHOMIUS

The Life of Saint Pachomius and His Disciples, translated with an introduction by Armand Veilleux, Monk of Mistassini, foreword by Adalbert de Vogüé; 3 vols., pp. 1:430–32, 2:146–49, 439–40, 3:18–21. Kalamazoo, Mich.: Cistercian Publications, 1980.

St. Pachomius was born about 292 in Egypt and is considered the founder of "communal" monasticism, essentially organizing hermits into groups, the first being Tabennesi, around 320, growing into several thousand monks by his death in 346. The Rule was a compilation of regulations which were added to and augmented by Pachomius' successors, therefore no sure date is given for their compilation. The Pachomian vision of the ascetic life includes the benefits of the *Koinonia*, Greek for "community." In these selections, Pachomius illuminates communal benefits while highlighting the goal of the life of a monk. Also note the role of the abbot as leader of the community, the spiritual father giving guidance and imparting spiritual wisdom. Both St. Basil and St. Benedict drew from this Rule in setting forth their own more famous ones.

10. Then one by one, people from the surrounding villages came to him. They built dwellings for themselves in the place where he had retired and they gathered there to live the anchoritic life. Together they constituted a small group of men.

11. When he saw the brothers gathering around him, he established for them the following rule: Each should be self-supporting and manage his own affairs, but they would provide their share of all their material needs either for food or to provide hospitality to the strangers who came to them, for they all ate together. They brought their share to him and he administered it. They did this freely and voluntarily so that he could see to all their needs, because they considered him trustworthy and because he was their father after God. This regulation he

established was adapted to their weakness, in line with what the Apostle says, "To the weak I became weak, that I might gain the weak" (1 Cor. 9:22). And writing to the Corinthians he says also, "I fed you with milk, not with solid food, for you were not yet ready for it" (1 Cor. 3:2). He proceeded this way because he could see that they were not yet ready to bind themselves together in a perfect *Koinonia* like that of the believers which Acts describes: "They were one heart and one soul and everything they owned was held in common; not one of them said that anything he possessed was his own" (Acts 4:32). As the Apostle says again, "Do not forget communion and good works, for these are sacrifices that please God" (Heb. 13:16).

12. Our father Pachomius nourished them as well as he could, as it is written, "A righteous father gives good food" (Prov. 23:24). That which he received from them according to this regulation, he administered in conformity with all their regulations. If they happened to bring him fish or other provisions, he received them and prepared them for them. Then when he had finished preparing their food and had given it to them to eat, if he has fasted the preceding day, he would put a bit of salt in his hand and would then eat bread on [the salt]. This is how he always dealt with them, becoming their servant according to the covenant he had made before God, as Paul says, "For free thou I was in everything, to all I have made myself a servant that I might win more" (1 Cor. 9:19).

13. Seeing his humility and obligingness, they treated him with contempt and great irreverence because of the lack of integrity of their hearts toward God. If he told them once to take care of some need they had, they would contradict him openly and insult him, saying, "We will not obey you." He did not punish them, however, but on the contrary, he bore with them with great patience saying, "They will see my humility and affliction and they will return to God reforming themselves and fearing him." This he did also according to what Paul says, "A servant of the Lord must not quarrel, but be kind to everyone, instructing and enduring evil, gently instructing those who dispute, so that God might give them repentance, that they might know the truth and recover from

the snare of the devil, to whose will they are held captive" (2 Tim. 2:24–26).

The Bohairic Life of Pachomius

105. . . . "I will show you as well that the honor and the glory of the men of the *Koinonia*, who have a good way of life together with the excellence of the toils they impose on themselves, are superior to those of men who lead the anchoritic life. I will show you also that the ruin, the falls, and the loss of those who do not walk correctly in the *Koinonia* give rise to greater scandal than among those who lead the anchoritic life. Indeed, it is like a trader who sails on the sea and rivers in all kinds of weather. If he escapes the sea's danger he will get very rich; but if his boat goes down, not only will his wealth be lost, but his life too and his remembrance will be lost forever. At the same time, listen to the interpretation: he who makes progress in the *Koinonia* with purity, obedience, humility, and submissiveness, and puts no stumbling-block or scandal before anyone by his words or by his acts, that one will grow rich forever in imperishable and enduring riches. But should he be negligent, and should a soul be scandalized by him and perish from it, woe to that man; not only has he lost his soul and the troubles he took on himself, but he also will have to render an account to God for that soul he scandalized.

"About those who lead the anchoritic life, listen, and I will teach you their parable. It is like a merchant selling bread or vegetables or anything else of that kind in the market-place. He is not going to get rich on such a daily gain, but neither will he be in want of any of this world's material things. So it is with an ascetic leading the anchoritic life. He does not bear the responsibility of other ascetics, but neither does he see those who practice exercises—a thing which would incite him to imitate their actions and the excellent practices they perform in order to do the same himself. Well, such a man will not rank high in the kingdom of heaven, but neither will he be deprived of eternal life, because of the purity of the *ascesis* he has practiced. The reward for the fasts, prayers, and exercises he has performed in Christ's name and for the love and the fear he bore him will be paid him by Christ tremendously multiplied in the age to come, in his kingdom.

"Again I will instruct you by a parable about the brothers who are the lowliest in the *Koinonia*, who do not give themselves up to great practices and to an excessive *ascesis*, but walk simply in the purity of their bodies and according to the established rules with obedience and obligingness. In the view of people who live as anchorites, their way of life does not seem perfect and they are looked upon as the lowliest. Truly, it is like favorite servants of the king and his favorite eunuchs: they have greater freedom of movement in the palace than the powerful who are under the king's orders and who cannot get at the king unless they have themselves announced to him by the eunuchs. So it is with those others who are considered the lowliest in the *Koinonia*, and will be found perfect in the law of Christ (cf. Gal. 6:2) because of their steadfastness. They practice exercises in all submissiveness according to God. They are also far superior to those who live as anchorites, for they walk in the obligingness the Apostle walked in, as it is written, 'By the love of the Spirit, be servants of one another in a kindly spirit and in all patience before our Lord Jesus' (cf. Gal. 5:13; Eph. 4:2, 32)."

Fragment VI

25. He acted like a true shepherd who takes care of his flock. The weak he nurtured in the pastures of righteousness. The vicious he fettered with the bonds of the Gospel. Those who went astray he brought back to the sheepfold. The fat and the first born, he offered on the altar as sacrifices to the Lord for Him to smell their fragrance, following the example of Noah who took clean animals and birds and offered them on the altar, and God smelled the fragrance (Gen. 8:20–21). Likewise Paul says, "We are the fragrance of the Christ of God" (2 Cor. 2:15). Pachomius strove in every way to avoid the reproach that the prophet Ezechiel addressed to the shepherds (Ezek. 34). Indeed, the sheep, which the Lord had brought together for him, he nurtured according to the Apostle's command, "Instruct the ignorant, exhort the faint-hearted, help the weak, be patient with everyone" (1 Thess. 5:14). And truly [the Apostle] urged the sheep of the Lord to eat good food, so that they would be a fragrance for the Lord as when he said, "I exhort you, my brothers, to offer your bodies as a living sacrifice, holy and pleasing to

God" (Rom. 12:1), not only to be a fragrance from the purity of their bodies but also from the purity of their hearts, as David says, "The sacrifice to God is a broken spirit" (Ps. 51[50]:17), and he begged them to become by their mouths a sacrifice of blessing.

The Instructions of Saint Pachomius [PK, III:18–21]

16. And now, my son, if you take God as your hope, he will be your help in the time of your anguish; "for anyone who comes to God must believe that he exists and that he rewards those who search for him" (Heb. 11:6). These words were written for us, that we may believe in God and do battle, great and little, by fasts, prayers, and other religious practices. God will not forget even the saliva that has dried in your mouth as a result of fasting. On the contrary, everything will be returned to you at the moment of your anguish. Only humble yourself in all things, hold back your word even if you understand the whole affair. Do not quietly acquire the habit of abusing; on the contrary, joyfully put up with every trial. For if you knew the honor that results from trials you would not pray to be delivered from them, because it is preferable for you to pray, to weep, and to sigh until you are saved, rather than to relax and be led off a captive. O man, what are you doing in Babylon? "You have grown old in an alien land" (Bar. 3:10) because you did not submit to the test and because your relations with God are not proper. Therefore, brother, you must not relax.

17. Maybe you are a bit forgetful. But your enemies have not fallen asleep, and night and day they do not forget to set traps for you. Do not seek after honors, then, so you will not be humiliated to the great joy of your enemies. Seek rather humility, "for he who exalts himself will be humbled, and he who humbles himself will be exalted" (Matt. 23:12). If you cannot get along alone, join another who is living according to the Gospel of Christ, and you will make progress with him. Either listen, or submit to one who listens; either be strong and be called Elijah, or obey the strong and be called Elisha. For obeying Elijah, Elisha received a double share of Elijah's spirit.

18. If you wish to live among men, imitate Abraham, Lot, Moses, and Samuel. If you wish to live in the desert, all the prophets have led the way there before you. Be like them, "wandering in the deserts, valleys and caves of the earth" (Heb. 11:38), plunged in misery, trials, and affliction. It is said again, "The shadow of the parched and the spirit of the maltreated will bless you" (Isa. 25:4). And then, for the thief on the cross—the one who spoke a word—the Lord forgave his sins and received him into paradise (Luke 23:40–43). See what honor will be yours if you have steadfastness in the face of trial or of the spirit of fornication, or the spirit of pride, or any other passion. Do battle against diabolic passions, not to follow them, and Jesus will grant you what he has promised. Keep from negligence; it is the mother of all the vices.

19. My son, flee concupiscence (cf. Ecclus. 5:2). It beclouds the mind and prevents it from coming to know the mystery of God (cf. Matt. 12:11). It makes you alien to the language of the Spirit and prevents you from carrying the Cross of Christ (cf. Matt. 10:38; Luke 9:23; 14:27). It does not permit the heart to be attentive to honoring God. Keep from the belly's inclination, which makes you alien to the goods of paradise. Keep from impurity, which irritates God and his angels.

20. My son, turn to God, and love him (cf. Ecclus. 17:25). Flee the enemy and despise him. May the graces of God come your way and may you inherit the blessing of Judah, son of Jacob. It is said, "Judah, your brothers shall praise you, your hands will be on the back of your enemies, and the sons of your father shall be your servants" (Gen. 49:8). Keep away from pride, for it is the beginning of every evil. And the beginning of pride is keeping your distance from God, and hardening the heart is what follows. If you guard against this, your resting place will be the heavenly Jerusalem. If the Lord loves you and gives you glory, keep from becoming proud; on the contrary, persevere in humility and you will abide in the glory that God has given you. Watch out, be vigilant, for "blessed is the one who is found watching, because he will be set over the possessions of his master" (Matt. 24:46–47), and he will enter into the kingdom with gladness. The friends of the bridegroom will love him, because they have found him keeping watch over his vineyard.

21. My son, be merciful in all things, for it is written, "Strive to be presented to God as having come through trial, like a workman who fears no shame" (2 Tim. 2:15). Approach God as one who sows and reaps, and into your granary you will gather God's goods. Do not pray with much show, in the manner of hypocrites, but give up your whims and do what you do for God, acting thus for your own salvation. If a passion arouses you, whether it is love of money, jealousy, or hatred and the other passions, watch out, "have the heart of a lion" (2 Sam. 17:10), a strong heart. Fight against them, make them disappear like Sihon, Og, and all the kings of the Amorites. May the beloved Son, the Only-begotten, Jesus the king, fight for you, and may you inherit enemy towns. Still, toss all pride far from your side, and be valiant. Look: when Joshua [son] of Nun was valiant, God delivered his enemies into his hands. If you are fainthearted, you become a stranger to the law of God. Faintheartedness fills you with pretexts for laziness, mistrust, and negligence, until you are destroyed. Be lion-hearted and shout, you as well, "Who can separate us from the love of God?" (Rom. 8:35). And say, "Though my outer self may dissolve, still my inner self is renewed from day to day" (2 Cor. 4:16).

SAINT BASIL: THE LONG RULES

From *The Fathers of the Church: A New Translation*, trans. M. Monica Wagner (Washington, D.C.: Catholic University of America Press, 1950; reprint, 1962, 1970).

Saint Basil the Great of Caesarea (ca. 330–79) is the author of the first major Rule with which we are concerned, *The Long Rules*, also known as *The Longer Rules for Monks*. Basil's Rule was composed between 358 and 364, and the form used here, *The Long Rules*, contains a preface plus a series of fifty-five questions and answers in catechism fashion. (There is another form of this Rule that consists of 313 questions and answers and is usually called *The Shorter Rules for Monks*.) Our selections begin with question three, which emphasizes charity, or love within the community. This is followed by questions and answers on the duty of *caritas*, or love, to all, one's proper attitude toward the Lord, the benefits in renunciation of the world and seclusion, work and prayer, on authority and obedience, and finally on acceptance or nonacceptance of these Rules.

Q[uestion] 3. Of charity toward one's neighbor.
It would be logical to take up next the commandment which is second both in order and emphasis.
R[esponse]. We have already said above that the law [of God] develops and maintains the powers existing in germ within us. And since we are directed to love our neighbor as ourselves, let us consider whether we have received from the Lord the power to fulfill this commandment also. Who does not know that man is a civilized and gregarious animal, neither savage nor a lover of solitude! Nothing, indeed, is so compatible with our nature as living in society and in dependence upon one another and as loving our own kind. Now, the Lord Himself gave to us the seeds of these qualities in anticipation of His requiring in due time their fruits, for He says: "A new commandment I give unto you: that you love one another" (John 13:34). Moreover, wishing to animate our soul to the observance of this commandment, He did not require signs

or wonders as the means of recognizing His disciples (although He gave the power of working these also in the Holy Spirit), but He says: "By this shall all men know that you are my disciples, if you have love one for another" (John 13:35). Further, He establishes so close a connection between the two great commandments that benefit conferred upon the neighbor is transferred to Himself: "For I was hungry," He says, "and you gave me to eat" (Matt. 25:35), and so on, adding: "as long as you did it to one of these my least brethren, you did it to me" (Matt. 25:40).

It is, accordingly, possible to keep the second commandment by observing the first, and by means of the second we are led back to the first. He who loves the Lord loves his neighbor in consequence. "If anyone love me," said the Lord, "he will keep my commandments" (John 14:23); and again, He says: "This is my commandment, that you love one another as I have loved you" (John 15:12). On the other hand, he who loves his neighbor fulfills the love he owes to God, for He accepts this favor as shown to Himself. Wherefore, Moses, that faithful servant of God, manifested such great love for his brethren as to wish his name to be struck off the book of God in which it was inscribed, if the sin of his people were not pardoned (Exod. 32:32). Paul, also, desiring to be, like Christ, an exchange for the salvation of all, dared to pray that he might be an anathema from Christ for the sake of his brethren who were his kinsmen according to the flesh (Rom. 9:3). Yet, at the same time, he knew that it was impossible for him to be estranged from God through his having rejected His favor for love of Him and for the sake of that great commandment; moreover, he knew that he would receive in return much more than he gave. For the rest, what has been said thus far offers sufficient proof that the saints did attain to this measure of love for their neighbor.

Q[uestion] 4. Of the fear of God.
R[esponse]. For those newly entered upon the way of piety, the basic discipline acquired through fear is more profitable, according to the counsel of Solomon, wisest of men: "The fear of the Lord is the beginning of wisdom" (Prov. 1:7). But, for you who have, as it were, passed through your infancy in Christ and no longer require milk but are able to be perfected according to the inner man by the solid nourishment of doctrine (Heb. 5:13–14), loftier precepts are needed whereby the whole

truth of the love which is in Christ is brought to fulfillment. But, manifestly, you must be on your guard lest the superabundance of the gifts of God make you liable to a harsher judgment if you are ungrateful to the Giver; for He says: "to whom they have committed much, of him they will demand the more" (Luke 12:48). . . .

Q[uestion] 6. Concerning the necessity of living in retirement.
R[esponse]. A secluded and remote habitation also contributes to the removal of distraction from the soul. Living among those who are unscrupulous and disdainful in their attitude toward an exact observance of the commandments is dangerous, as is shown by the following words of Solomon: "Be not a friend to an angry man and do not walk with a furious man; lest perhaps thou learn his ways and take snares to thy soul" (Prov. 22:24–25). The words of the Apostle, "Go out from among them and be ye separate, saith the Lord" (2 Cor. 6:17), bear also upon this point. Consequently, that we may not receive incitements to sin through our eyes and ears and become imperceptibly habituated to it, and that the impress and form, so to speak, of what is seen and heard may not remain in the soul unto its ruin, and that we may be able to be constant in prayer, we should before all things else seek to dwell in a retired place. In so doing, we should be able to overcome our former habits whereby we lived as strangers to the precepts of Christ (and it is no mean struggle to gain the mastery over one's wonted manner of acting, for custom maintained throughout a long period takes on the force of nature), and we could wipe away the stains of sin by assiduous prayer and persevering meditation on the will of God. It is impossible to gain proficiency in this meditation and prayer, however, while a multitude of distractions is dragging the soul about and introducing into it anxieties about the affairs of this life. Could anyone, immersed in these cares, ever fulfill that command: "If any man will come after me, let him deny himself" (Luke 9:23). For, we must deny ourselves and take up the Cross of Christ and thus follow Him. Now, self-denial involves the entire forgetfulness of the past and surrender of one's will—surrender which it is very difficult, not to say quite impossible, to achieve while living in the promiscuity customary in the world. And in addition, the social intercourse demanded by such a life is even an obstacle

to taking up one's cross and following Christ. Readiness to die for Christ, the mortification of one's members on this earth, preparedness for every danger which might befall us on behalf of Christ's Name, detachment from this life—this it is to take up one's cross; and we regard the obstacles springing from the habits of life in society as major impediments thereto.

And in addition to all the other obstacles, which are many, the soul in looking at the crowd of other offenders does not, in the first place, have time to become aware of its own sins and to afflict itself by penance for its errors; on the contrary, by comparison with those who are worse, it takes on, besides, a certain deceptive appearance of righteousness. Secondly, through the disturbances and occupations which life in society naturally engenders, the soul, being drawn away from the more worthy remembrance of God, pays the penalty of finding neither joy nor gladness in God and of not relishing the delights of the Lord or tasting the sweetness of His words, so as to be able to say: "I remembered God and was delighted" (Ps. 76:4), and "How sweet are thy words to my palate! more than honey to my mouth" (Ps. 118:103). Worse still, it becomes habituated to a disregard and a complete forgetfulness of His judgments, than which no more fatal misfortune could befall it.

Q[uestion] 7. On the necessity of living in the company of those who are striving for the same objective—that of pleasing God—and the difficulty and hazards of living as a solitary.
Since your words have convinced us that it is dangerous to live in company with those who hold the commandments of God in light regard, we consider it logical to inquire whether one who retires from society should live in solitude or with brethren who are of the same mind and who have set before themselves the same goal, that is, the devout life.
R[esponse]. . . . Community life offers more blessings than can be fully and easily enumerated. It is more advantageous than the solitary life both for preserving the goods bestowed on us by God and for warding off the external attacks of the Enemy. If any should happen to grow heavy with that sleep which is unto death and which we have been instructed by David to avert with prayer: "Enlighten my eyes that I never sleep in death" (Ps. 12:4), the awakening induced by those who are already on

watch is the more assured. For the sinner, moreover, the withdrawal from his sin is far easier if he fears the shame of incurring censure from many acting together—to him, indeed, might be applied the words: "To him who is such a one, this rebuke is sufficient which is given by many" (2 Cor. 2:6) and for the righteous man, there is a great and full satisfaction in the esteem of the group and in their approval of his conduct. If in the mouth of two or three witnesses, every word shall stand (Matt. 18:16), he who performs a good action will be far more surely corroborated by the testimony of many. Besides these disadvantages, the solitary life is fraught with other perils. The first and greatest is that of self-satisfaction. Since the solitary has no one to appraise his conduct, he will think he has achieved the perfection of the precept. Secondly, because he never tests his state of soul by exercise, he will not recognize his own deficiencies nor will he discover the advance he may have made in his manner of acting, since he will have removed all practical occasion for the observance of the commandments.

Wherein will he show his humility, if there is no one with whom he may compare and so confirm his own greater humility? Wherein will he give evidence of his compassion, if he has cut himself off from association with other persons? And how will he exercise himself in long-suffering, if no one contradicts his wishes? If anyone says that the teaching of the Holy Scripture is sufficient for the amendment of his ways, he resembles a man who learns carpentry without ever actually doing a carpenter's work or a man who is instructed in metal-working but will not reduce theory to practice. To such a one the Apostle would say: "Not the hearers of the law are just before God, but the doers of the law shall be justified" (Rom. 2:13). Consider, further, that the Lord by reason of His excessive love for man was not content with merely teaching the word, but, so as to transmit to us clearly and exactly the example of humility in the perfection of charity, girded Himself and washed the feet of the disciples (John 13:5). Whom, therefore, will you wash? To whom will you minister? In comparison with whom will you be the lowest, if you live alone? How, moreover, in a solitude, will that good and pleasant thing be accomplished, the dwelling of brethren together in one habitation (Ps. 132:1) which the Holy Spirit likens to ointment emitting its fragrance from the head of the high priest (Ps. 132:2)?

So it is an arena for the combat, a good path of progress, continual discipline, and a practicing of the Lord's commandments, when brethren dwell together in community. This kind of life has as its aim the glory of God according to the command of our Lord Jesus Christ, who said: "So let your light shine before men that they may see your good works and glorify your Father who is in heaven" (Matt. 5:16). It maintains also the practice characteristic of the saints, of whom it is recorded in the Acts: "And all they that believed were together and had all things common" (Acts 2:44) and again: "And the multitude of believers had but one heart and one soul; neither did anyone say that aught of the things which he possessed was his own, but all things were common unto them" (Acts 4:32). . . .

Q[uestion] 41. Of authority and obedience.
R[esponse]. Even in the case of authorized trades, the individual ought not be permitted to follow the one he is skilled in or the one he wishes to learn, but that for which he may be judged suited. He who denies himself and completely sets aside his own wishes does not do what he wills but what he is directed to do. Nor, indeed, does reason permit that he himself make choice of what is good and useful, since he has irrevocably turned over the disposal of himself to others who will appoint the task for which they in the Lord's Name may find him suited. Whoever chooses a task conformed to his personal wish brings accusation against himself; first, of self-gratification; second, of preferring a certain trade for the sake of worldly renown or hope of gain, or some such reason, or of choosing the easier course out of sloth and indifference. To be guilty of such faults, however, is an indication that a man is not yet free from evil passions. Nor, to be sure, has he practiced self- denial, since in his eagerness to give full play to his own impulses he does not give up the things of this world, being still held captive by prospects of gain and renown. Neither has he mortified his members which are upon the earth (Col. 3:5), since he does not endure fatigue in his labors, but betrays his own willfulness by regarding his private judgment as more reliable than the appraisal of him on the part of several others. One who is master of a trade that is in no way objectionable to the community ought not abandon it, however, for to deem of no account that which

is at one's immediate disposal is the sign of a fickle mind and an unstable will. And if a man is unskilled, he should not of himself take up a trade, but should accept the one approved by his superiors, so as to safeguard obedience in all things. Now, just as it has been shown to be unfitting that one should rely upon oneself, so it is forbidden also to refuse to submit to the decision of others. And if one is adept in a trade that is unacceptable to the community, he should be ready to renounce it in proof that he has no affection for anything in this world. To follow personal preference is, in the words of the Apostle, the act of one who has no hope (1 Thess. 4:12); but to be obedient in all things is worthy of approbation, since the same Apostle praises certain persons because "they gave their own selves first to the Lord, then also to us, by the will of God" (2 Cor. 8:5). For the rest, everyone should be devoted to his own trade, applying himself to it enthusiastically and accomplishing it blamelessly with ready zeal and careful attention, as if God were his overseer, so that he may ever be able to say in all honesty: "Behold, as the eyes of servants are on the hands of their masters, so are our eyes unto the Lord our God" (Ps. 122:2); but one should not work now at one kind of task, now at another.

We are incapable by nature of following successfully a number of pursuits at the same time; to finish one task with diligent care is more beneficial than to undertake many and not complete them. If the mind is distracted by several occupations and passes from one to another, besides the fact that nothing is perfectly finished, such procedure betokens levity of character as already present or, if not that, as being inculcated. In case of necessity, however, one who has the ability may assist in other trades besides his own. Yet this also should not be done of one's own volition, but only upon being summoned, for we should have recourse to this expedient at the call of emergency and not on our own initiative; just as, in the case of our bodily members, we support ourselves with the hand when the foot is limping. Again, as it is not good to take up a trade on one's personal initiative, so, not to accept one that is appointed deserves censure, to prevent the vice of contumacy from being fostered or the limits of docility and obedience from being transgressed. Furthermore, the care of tools devolves, first of all, upon the artisan of each trade. If it should happen, however, that some oversight occur, those who first notice it should take the proper steps, on the ground that the tools are possessed by all in common; although their use is a private matter, the benefit from them is for all, and to regard the instruments of another's trade with disdainful indifference betrays a want of community spirit. It is not fitting, moreover, for those who follow trades to exercise such authority over their tools as not to permit the superior of the community to use them for whatever purpose he wishes, or that they should of themselves take the liberty of selling or exchanging them, or getting rid of them in any other way or of acquiring others in addition to those they have. How could he who has irrevocably chosen not to be master even of his own hands and who has consigned to another the direction of their activity, how could he be consistent in maintaining full authority over the tools of his trade, arrogating to himself the dignity of mastership over them?

THE CONFERENCES OF CASSIAN

Selections from John Cassian, *The Conferences*, translated and annotated by Boniface Ramsey. In Ancient Christian Writers: The Works of the Fathers in Translation, 57. New York/Mahwah, N. J.: Paulist Press, 1997.

John Cassian's (ca. 367–ca. 435) influence on monastic life in the West cannot be overstated. While not a Rule per se, Cassian's "conferences" provide vital information on the goals of the monastic life and therefore must be represented. In his conferences, composed sometime between 426–29, Cassian guides his audience into the richness of the monastic life as he witnessed while living with Egyptian monastics in the last decades of the fourth century. Cassian is said to have translated the principles and ideals of the East into the culture of the West, thereby influencing generations of Western monks in the spiritual life found in the monastic community. The monastic historian C. H. Lawrence says that, in Cassian, the Western monastic movement found its theological foundations (*Medieval monasticism*, 17). In this selection, Cassian picks up on the themes of personal reformation of the image of God through the physical and spiritual exercises modeled by Martha and Mary, images that will become commonplace in monastic writings. Also, Cassian emphasizes charity—or better translated, love—as one of the central goals of communal monasticism, loving purely, which truly leads to perfection.

Preface to the First Part of the Conferences of John Cassian

In this respect, now that I have settled in a harbor of silence, a vast sea lies before me, inasmuch as I am daring to commit to writing something on the institutes and teaching of such men. As the solitary life is greater and more sublime than that of the cenobia, and the contemplation of God—upon which those inestimable men were ever intent—than the active life that is led in communities, so must the bark of a limited understanding be tossed about amidst the dangers of deeper waters. Your part, then, is to help our efforts with your devout prayers, lest the holy material that is to be presented be imperiled by us because of inexpert, albeit faithful, words, or again lest our simplicity be overwhelmed in the depths of this same material.

Consequently, let us proceed from the external and visible life of the monks, which we have summarized in the previous books, to the invisible character of the inner man, and from the practice of the canonical prayers let our discourse arise to the unceasing nature of that perpetual prayer which the Apostle commands (1 Thess. 5:17). Thus the person who has read the previous work and is worthy of the name of that spiritual Jacob because of the supplanting of the carnal vices (cf. Gen. 27:36) may now—taking up not so much my own institutes as those of the fathers and passing over to the deserts and as it were the dignity of Israel (cf. Gen. 32:29), thanks to an insight into the divine purity— be also similarly taught what must be observed at this summit of perfection. And so let your prayers obtain from him who has judged us worthy to see them and to be their disciples and friends the bestowal of a complete recollection of those same traditions and a pleasing mode of expression. Thus, while explaining those things as wholly and as completely as we received them, we may be able to put before you those very same men, embodied somehow in their own institutes and (what is more) speaking in the Latin tongue.

Before anything else, we want the reader of these conferences as well as of the previous volumes to be advised that if perhaps he thinks, by reason of his status and chosen orientation or from the point of view of ordinary custom and way of life, that there are things in these books that are impossible or hard, he should not judge them by the standard of his own ability but according to the dignity of the speakers, whose zeal and chosen orientation he should first mentally grasp, since those who have truly died to this world's life are bound by no love for kinsfolk nor by any ties of worldly deeds. Finally, let him also consider the kinds of places in which they are living. Thanks to them, they who have established themselves in the vastest solitude and are separated from the companionship of all mortal beings, thereby possessing spiritual enlightenment, contemplate and proclaim things that will perhaps seem impossible to those who are unpracticed and ignorant by reason

of their condition and their mediocre behavior. In this regard, however, if anyone wishes to give a true opinion and desires to see whether
these things can be fulfilled, let him first hasten to seize upon their
chosen orientation with similar zeal and by a similar way of life. Only
then will he realize that what seemed beyond human capacity is not
only possible but even most sweet.

But now let us get on to their conferences and institutes.

First Conference of Abba Moses:
On the Goal and the End of the Monk

When I, along with the holy Abba Germanus (with whom I was so
closely befriended from the very time of our basic training and the
beginnings of our spiritual soldiery, both in the cenobium and in the
desert, that everyone used to say, by way of pointing out the identity of
our companionship and our chosen orientation, that we were one mind
and soul inhabiting two bodies), was looking in the desert of Skete,
where the most experienced fathers of the monks and every perfection
dwelled, for Abba Moses, who in the midst of those splendid flowers
gave off a particularly sweet odor because of both his practical and his
contemplative virtue, and, as together we were tearfully begging for an
edifying word from that abba, since we were eager to be thoroughly
instructed by him, he finally began to speak, worn out by our pleading.
(In fact we had been quite aware of his inflexible attitude, such that he
would never consent to open the portal of perfection except to those
who faithfully desired it and who sought it in utter contrition of heart.
Otherwise, if he disclosed it without further ado to those who were unwilling or to those whose desire was not a consuming one, he would
seem to be committing either the vice of boasting or the crime of
betrayal by pandering important things, which should only be known
to those seeking perfection, to the unworthy and to those who would
receive them disdainfully.)

II.1. "All the arts and disciplines," he said, "have a certain *scopos* or goal,
and a *telos*, which is the end that is proper to them, on which the lover
of any art sets his gaze and for which he calmly and gladly endures every

labor and danger and expense. For the farmer, avoiding neither the torrid rays of the sun one time nor the frost and ice another, tirelessly tills the soil and subdues the unyielding clumps of earth with his frequent plowing, and all the while he keeps his *scopos* in mind: that, once it has been cleared of all the briars and every weed has been uprooted, by his hard work he may break the soil into something as fine as sand. In no other way does he believe that he will achieve his end, which is to have a rich harvest and an abundant crop, with which he may thenceforth both live his life in security and increase his substance."

2. "Laboring in dedicated fashion, he even willingly removes produce from his well-stocked barns and puts it in crumbling ditches, not thinking of present diminution when he reflects on the future harvest. Likewise, those who are accustomed to engage in commerce do not fear the uncertain behavior of the sea, nor are they afraid of any risks, since they are spurred on by winged hope to the end of profit. Neither are those who are inflamed by worldly military ambition, seeking as they do the end of honors and power, conscious of calamities and the dangers of their long treks, nor are they crushed by present fatigue and wars, since they wish to attain the end of high rank that they have set for themselves.

3. "Our profession also has a *scopos* proper to itself and its own end, on behalf of which we tirelessly and even gladly expend all our efforts. For its sake the hunger of fasting does not weary us, the exhaustion of keeping vigil delights us, and the continual reading of and meditating on Scripture does not sate us. Even the unceasing labor, the being stripped and deprived of everything and, too, the horror of this vast solitude do not deter us. Without doubt it is for its sake that you yourselves have spurned the affection of relatives, despised your homeland and the delights of the world and have journeyed through so many foreign parts in order to come to us, men rude and unlearned, living harshly in the desert. Tell me, therefore," he asked, "what is your goal and what is your end, which drives you to endure all these things so willingly?"

III. And when he insisted on having our answer to this question, we replied that we bore all these things for the sake of the kingdom of heaven.

IV. 1. On hearing this he said: "Good! You have spoken well about your end. But before anything else you should know what ought to be our *scopos* or our goal, by constantly clinging to which we may be able to attain our end." And when we had in all simplicity confessed our ignorance, he added: "As I have said, in every art and discipline a certain *scopos* takes precedence. This is the soul's goal and the mind's constant intention, which cannot be maintained nor the final end of the longed-for fruit arrived at except by an encompassing diligence and perseverance.

2. For, as I have said, the farmer who has as his end a secure and comfortable life, thanks to his fruitful lands, pursues his *scopos* or goal by clearing his field of all the briars and emptying it of every unfruitful weed, and he does not believe that he will achieve his end of peaceful affluence in any other way than as it were by first possessing by toil and hope what he desires to have the actual use of. Neither does the businessman lay aside his desire of procuring merchandise, by which he may more easily get rich, since he would long for money in vain if he did not choose the means that would get him to it. And those who want to be honored with any of this world's honors first decide on what office or position they should devote themselves to, so that within the normal course of events they may also be able to attain the final end of the sought-after dignity.

3. Hence, too, the end of our course is the kingdom of God. But we should inquire carefully into the nature of our goal. If we have not in similar fashion grasped this we shall be wearied fruitlessly by our toil, because if the road is uncharted, then those who undertake the hardships of the journey will have nothing to show for it." As we listened to this in amazement, the old man continued: "The end of our profession, as we have said, is the kingdom of God or the kingdom of heaven; but the goal or *scopos* is purity of heart, without which it is impossible for anyone to reach that end.

4. Fixing our gaze on this goal, then, as on a definite mark, we shall take the most direct route. If our attention should wander somewhat from it we shall at once return to its contemplation, accurately correcting

ourselves as if by a kind of rule that will always measure all our efforts and recall them to this one mark, if our mind should have deviated ever so slightly from the proposed direction." . . .

V. 3. "Whatever therefore can direct us to this *scopos*, which is purity of heart, is to be pursued with all our strength, but whatever deters us from this is to be avoided as dangerous and harmful. For it is for its sake that we do and endure everything, for its sake that family, homeland, honors, wealth, the pleasures of this world, and every enjoyment are disdained—so that perpetual purity of heart may be kept.

4. With this goal always set before us, therefore, our actions and thoughts are ordered to attaining it in the most direct way. If it is not constantly fixed before our eyes, not only will all our labors be rendered equally useless and shaky and be made vain and profitless, but all sorts of confusing thoughts will be aroused as well. It is inevitable that the mind which does not have a place to turn to or any stable base will undergo change from hour to hour and from minute to minute due to the variety of its distractions, and by the things that come to it from outside it will be continually transformed into whatever occurs to it at any given moment."

VII. 1. "For the sake of this, then, everything is to be done and desired. For its sake solitude is to be pursued; for its sake we know that we must undertake fasts, vigils, labors, bodily deprivation, readings, and other virtuous things, so that by them we may be able to acquire and keep a heart untouched by any harmful passion, and so that by taking these steps we may be able to ascend to the perfection of love."

"It behooves us, then, to carry out the things that are secondary—namely, fasts, vigils, the solitary life, and meditation on Scripture—for the sake of the principal scopes, which is purity of heart or love, rather than for their sake to neglect this principal virtue which, as long as it remains integral and intact, will prevent anything bad from happening to us whenever one of the things that are secondary has to be omitted out of necessity. For it will be of no use to have fulfilled everything if this primary object, for the sake of attaining which all things are to be pursued, has been lost. . . .

3. It is for this reason that a person hastens to acquire for himself and to assemble the implements of a given art—not so that he may possess them without using them, nor so that he may consider the enjoyment that he hopes for from them to consist in the mere possession of those tools, but so that by making use of them he may effectively master and lay hold of the end of that discipline, for which these are helps. Thus fasts, vigils, meditating on Scripture, and the being stripped and deprived of every possession are not perfection, but they are the tools of perfection. For the end of that discipline does not consist in these things; rather, it is by them that one arrives at the end.

4. In vain, therefore, will a person undertake these exercises who is satisfied with them as if they were the highest good and who fixes his heart's attention only on them and not on attaining the end, on account of which these other things are to be sought, and who makes every effort for the sake of virtue but, while indeed possessing the tools of the discipline, is ignorant of the end, in which all that is profitable is to be found. Whatever may disturb the purity and tranquillity of our mind, then, however useful and necessary it may appear, must be avoided as harmful. For in following this rule we shall be able both to avoid the byways of errors and distractions and, thanks to a clear direction, to arrive at the desired end."

VIII. 1. "This should be our principal effort, then; this should be constantly pursued as the fixed goal of our heart, so that our mind may always be attached to divine things and to God. Whatever is different from this, however great it may be, is nevertheless to be judged as secondary or even as base, and indeed as harmful. "Martha and Mary are very beautifully portrayed in the Gospel as examples of this attitude and manner of behavior. For although Martha was indeed devoting herself to a holy service, ministering as she was to the Lord himself and to his disciples, while Mary was intent only on spiritual teaching and was clinging to Jesus' feet, which she was kissing and anointing with the ointment of a good confession, yet it was she whom the Lord preferred, because she chose the better part, and one which could not be taken from her.

2. For as Martha was toiling with devout concern and was distracted with her work, she saw that she could not accomplish so large a task by herself, and she asked the Lord for her sister's help: "Does it not concern you that my sister has left me to serve by myself? Tell her to help me, then" (Luke 10:40). She was calling her not to a disreputable task, to be sure, but to a praiseworthy service. Yet what did she hear from the Lord? "Martha, Martha, you are concerned and troubled about many things, but few things are necessary, or even one. Mary has chosen the good part, which shall not be taken away from her" (Luke 10:41–42).

"You see, then, that the Lord considered the chief good to reside in theoria alone—that is, in divine contemplation.

3. Hence we take the view that the other virtues, although we consider them necessary and useful and good, are to be accounted secondary because they are all practiced for the purpose of obtaining this one thing. For when the Lord said: 'You are concerned and troubled about many things, but few things are necessary, or even one,' he placed the highest good not in carrying out some work, however praiseworthy, but in the truly simple and unified contemplation of him, declaring that 'few things' are necessary for perfect blessedness—namely, that theoria which is first established by reflecting on a few holy persons. Ascending from the contemplation of these persons, someone who is still advancing will arrive with his help at that which is also called 'one'—namely, the vision of God alone, so that, when he has gone beyond even the acts of holy persons and their wonderful works, he may be fed on the beauty and knowledge of God alone.

4. So it is that 'Mary has chosen the good part, which shall not be taken from her.' This too should be looked at more closely. For when he says: 'Mary has chosen the good part,' although he says nothing about Martha and certainly does not seem to reprimand her, nonetheless in praising the former he asserts that the latter occupies a lower position. Again, when he says: 'Which shall not be taken from her,' he indicates that the latter's position could be taken from her (for a person cannot uninterruptedly practice a ministry in the body), but he teaches that the zeal of the former can surely not come to an end in any age."

X. 5. "Those whose concern it is to press on to knowledge and to the purification of their minds have chosen, even while living in the present world, to give themselves to this objective with all their power and strength. While they are still dwelling in corruptible flesh they set themselves this charge, in which they will abide once corruption has been laid aside, when they come to that promise of the Lord, the Savior, which says: 'Blessed are the pure of heart, for they shall see God' (Matt. 5:8)."

Conference Ten: On Prayer

VII. 1. "For then will be brought to fruition in us that prayer of our Savior which he prayed to his Father on his disciples' behalf when he said: 'That the love with which you have loved me may be in them, and they in us' (John 17:26). And again: 'That all may be one, as you [*sic*] Father in me and I in you, that they also may be one in us' (John 17:21). Then that perfect love of God, by which 'he loved us first' (1 John 4:10), will have also passed into our heart's disposition upon the fulfillment of prayer of the Lord, which we believe can in no way be rendered void.

2. This will be the case when every love, every desire, effort, every undertaking, every thought of ours, everything that we live, that we speak, that we breathe, will be God, and when that unity which the father now has with the Son and which the son has with the Father will be carried over into our understanding and our mind, so that just as he loves us with a sincere and pure and indissoluble love, we too may be joined to him with a perpetual and inseparable love and so united with him that whatever we breathe, whatever we understand, whatever we speak, may be God. In him we shall attain, I say, to that end of which we spoke before, which the Lord longed to be fulfilled in us when he prayed: 'That all may be one as we are one, I in them and you in me, that they themselves may also be made perfect in Unity' (John 17:22–23). And again: 'Father, I wish that those whom you have given me may also be with me where I am' (John 17:24)."

Conference Eleven: On Perfection

VI. 1. Then the blessed Chaeremon said: "There are three things that restrain people from vice—namely, the fear of Gehenna or of present laws; or hope and desire for the kingdom of heaven; or a disposition for the good itself and a love of virtue.["] For we read that fear detests the contagion of evil: "The fear of the Lord hates wickedness" (Prov. 8:13). Hope, too, prevents the incursion of any vice, for "all who hope in him shall not fail" (Ps. 34:22). Love also dreads the destruction of sin, because "love never fails" (1 Cor. 13:8). And again: "Love covers a multitude of sins" (1 Pet. 4:8).

2. "Therefore the blessed Apostle includes the entire sum of salvation in the perfection of these three virtues, saying: "Now there abide faith, hope, love, these three" (1 Cor. 13:13). For it is faith that, through dread of future judgment and punishment, makes us refrain from the contagion of vice; hope that, calling our minds away from things present, despises all the pleasures of the body and waits for heavenly rewards; love that, inflaming us mentally with the love of Christ and with the fruit of spiritual virtue, makes us utterly despise whatever is contrary to those things."

"Although these three seem to tend to one end, inasmuch as they move us to abstain from what is unlawful, nonetheless they differ from one another by considerable degrees of excellence.

3. For the first two belong properly to those who are tending toward perfection and have not yet acquired a love of virtue, but the third belongs particularly to God and to those who have received in themselves the image and likeness of God. For only he does what is good who is moved not by fear or by the hope of reward but by a disposition for the good alone. As Solomon says: "The Lord has done all things for himself" (Prov. 16:4). For the sake of his own goodness he bestows an abundance of every good thing on the worthy and the unworthy, because he can neither be wearied by wrongdoing nor disturbed by human wickedness; he always abides perfectly good and by nature unchangeable."

THE RULE OF ST. AUGUSTINE

This translation by Robert Russell, O.S.A. (*The Rule of Our Holy Father St. Augustine: Bishop of Hippo*. Villanova, Penn.: Province of St. Thomas of Villanova, 1976) is based on the critical text of Luc Verheijen, O.S.A. (*La regle de saint Augustin*. Paris: Etudes Augustiniennes, 1967).

Written about the year 400, the *Rule of St. Augustine* does not establish a detailed way of life but simply, and with great flexibility, sets down a guide for life in common. Augustine (354–430), Bishop of Hippo, is said to have written the Rule for the canons of his Cathedral in Hippo, so that they could share in the communal life while still performing diocesan clerical duties taking them away from their Cathedral residence. The life described by Augustine has at its core a life lived in a community which seeks God through: renunciation of the world, communal and private prayer, and self-discipline. While not as influential in its own day, this Rule will become the foundation for several popular religious orders in future generations: the canons regular, the Order of Prémontre, and the Dominicans. It will also be incorporated into the *regula* for double monasteries such as the Gilbertines.

Purpose and Basis of Common Life
Before all else, dear brothers, love God and then your neighbor, because these are the chief commandments given to us.

1. The following are the precepts we order you living in the monastery to observe.

2. The main purpose for you having come together is to live harmoniously in your house, intent upon God in oneness of mind and heart.

3. Call nothing your own, but let everything be yours in common. Food and clothing shall be distributed to each of you by your superior, not equally to all, for all do not enjoy equal health, but rather according to

each one's need. For so you read in the Acts of the Apostles that they had all things in common and distribution was made to each one according to each one's need (Acts 4:32, 35).

4. Those who owned something in the world should be careful in wanting to share it in common once they have entered the monastery.

5. But they who owned nothing should not look for those things in the monastery that they were unable to have in the world. Nevertheless, they are to be given all that their health requires even if, during their time in the world, poverty made it impossible for them to find the very necessities of life. And those should not consider themselves fortunate because they have found the kind of food and clothing which they were unable to find in the world.

6. And let them not hold their heads high, because they associate with people whom they did not dare to approach in the world, but let them rather lift up their hearts and not seek after what is vain and earthly. Otherwise, monasteries will come to serve a useful purpose for the rich and not the poor, if the rich are made humble there and the poor are puffed up with pride.

7. The rich, for their part, who seemed important in the world, must not look down upon their brothers who have come into this holy brotherhood from a condition of poverty. They should seek to glory in the fellowship of poor brothers rather than in the reputation of rich relatives. They should neither be elated if they have contributed a part of their wealth to the common life, nor take more pride in sharing their riches with the monastery than if they were to enjoy them in the world. Indeed, every other kind of sin has to do with the commission of evil deeds, whereas pride lurks even in good works in order to destroy them. And what good is it to scatter one's wealth abroad by giving to the poor, even to become poor oneself, when the unhappy soul is thereby more given to pride in despising riches than it had been in possessing them?

8. Let all of you then live together in oneness of mind and heart, mutually honoring God in yourselves, whose temples you have become.

Chapter II
Prayer

1. Be assiduous in prayer (Col. 4:2), at the hours and times appointed.

2. In the Oratory no one should do anything other than that for which was intended and from which it also takes its name. Consequently, if there are some who might wish to pray there during their free time, even outside the hours appointed, they should not be hindered by those who think something else must be done there.

3. When you pray to God in Psalms and hymns, think over in your hearts the words that come from your lips.

4. Chant only what is prescribed for chant; moreover, let nothing be chanted unless it is so prescribed.

Chapter III
Moderation and Self-Denial

1. Subdue the flesh, so far as your health permits, by fasting and abstinence from food and drink. However, when someone is unable to fast, he should still take no food outside mealtimes unless he is ill.

2. When you come to table, listen until you leave to what is the custom to read, without disturbance or strife. Let not your mouths alone take nourishment but let your hearts too hunger for the words of God.

3. If those in more delicate health from their former way of life are treated differently in the matter of food, this should not be a source of annoyance to the others or appear unjust in the eyes of those who owe their stronger health to different habits of life. Nor should the healthier brothers deem them more fortunate for having food which they do not have, but rather consider themselves fortunate for having the good health which the others do not enjoy.

4. And if something in the way of food, clothing, and bedding is given to those coming to the monastery from a more genteel way of life, which is not given to those who are stronger, and therefore happier, then these latter ought to consider how far these others have come in passing from their life in the world down to this life of ours, though they have been unable to reach the level of frugality common to the stronger brothers. Nor should all want to receive what they see given in larger measure to the few, not as a token of honor, but as a help to support them in their weakness. This would give rise to a deplorable disorder—that in the monastery, where the rich are coming to bear as much hardship as they can, the poor are turning to a more genteel way of life.

5. And just as the sick must take less food to avoid discomfort, so too, after their illness, they are to receive the kind of treatment that will quickly restore their strength, even though they come from a life of extreme poverty. Their more recent illness has, as it were, afforded them what accrued to the rich as part of their former way of life. But when they have recovered their former strength, they should go back to their happier way of life which, because their needs are fewer, is all the more in keeping with God's servants. Once in good health, they must not become slaves to the enjoyment of food which was necessary to sustain them in their illness. For it is better to suffer a little want than to have too much.

Chapter VII
Governance and Obedience

1. The superior should be obeyed as a father with the respect due him so as not to offend God in his person, and, even more so, the priest who bears responsibility for you all.

2. But it shall pertain chiefly to the superior to see that these precepts are all observed and, if any point has been neglected, to take care that the transgression is not carelessly overlooked but is punished and corrected. In doing so, he must refer whatever exceeds the limit and power of his office, to the priest who enjoys greater authority among you.

3. The superior, for his part, must not think himself fortunate in his exercise of authority but in his role as one serving you in love. In your eyes he shall hold the first place among you by the dignity of his office, but in fear before God he shall be as the least among you. He must show himself as an example of good works toward all. Let him admonish the unruly, cheer the fainthearted, support the weak, and be patient toward all (1 Thess. 5:14). Let him uphold discipline while instilling fear. And though both are necessary, he should strive to be loved by you rather than feared, ever mindful that he must give an account of you to God.

4. It is by being more obedient, therefore, that you show mercy not only toward yourselves but also toward the superior whose higher rank among you exposes him all the more to greater peril.

Chapter VIII
Observance of the Rule

1. The Lord grant that you may observe all these precepts in a spirit of charity as lovers of spiritual beauty, giving forth the good odor of Christ in the holiness of your lives: not as slaves living under the law but as men living in freedom under grace.

2. And that you may see yourselves in this little book, as in a mirror, have it read to you once a week so as to neglect no point through forgetfulness. When you find that you are doing all that has been written, give thanks to the Lord, the Giver of every good. But when one of you finds that he has failed on any point, let him be sorry for the past, be on his guard for the future, praying that he will be forgiven his fault and not be led into temptation.

SAINT CAESARIUS OF ARLES

From *The Rule for Nuns of St. Caesarius of Arles: A Translation with a Critical Introduction*, translated and edited by Maria Cartias McCarthy. Studies in Mediaeval History, n.s. 16. Washington, D.C.: The Catholic University of America Press, 1960.

Bishop Caesarius of Arles (470–542) first wrote his *Rule for Nuns* in 512. He revised it several times and in 534 he authorized his final version and ordered that all earlier versions be destroyed. The version of 534 used here contains seventy-three chapters: the Rule proper makes up the first forty-seven chapters. The Latin title is *Regula sanctorum virginum*, which is variously translated/paraphrased into English as both *The Rule for Nuns* and *The Rules for Holy Virgins*.

The Rule for Nuns

Chapter 1. (Union with God through consecrated virginity)
HERE BEGIN THE RULES FOR HOLY VIRGINS
 Caesarius bishop, to our holy and highly venerated sisters in Christ, established in the monastery which by the inspiration and help of God we have founded. Because the Lord in His mercy has deigned to inspire and aid us to found a monastery for you, we have set down spiritual and holy counsels for you as to how you shall live in the monastery according to the prescriptions of the ancient Fathers. That, with the help of God, you may be able to keep them, as you abide unceasingly in your monastery cell, implore by assiduous prayer the visitation of the Son of God, so that afterwards you can say with confidence: "We have found Him Whom our soul has sought" (Cant. 3:1, 4). Hence I ask you, consecrated virgins and souls dedicated to God, who, with your lamps burning, await with secure consciences the coming of the Lord, that, as you know I have labored in the constructing of a monastery for you, you beg by your holy prayers to have me made a companion of your journey; so that when you happily enter the kingdom with the

holy and wise virgins, you may, by your suffrages, obtain for me that I remain not outside with the foolish. As you in your holiness pray for me and shine forth among the most precious gems of the Church, may the divine favor both fill you with present good things and render you worthy of the eternal.

Chapter 2. (Monastic life especially adapted to the needs of women)

And because many things in monasteries of women seem to differ from the customs of monks, we have chosen a few things from among many, according to which the elder religious can live under rule with the younger, and strive to carry out spiritually what they see to be especially adapted for their sex. These things first befit your holy souls: If a girl, leaving her parents, desire to renounce the world and enter the holy fold to escape the jaws of the spiritual wolves by the help of God, she must never, up to the time of her death, go out of the monastery, nor into the basilica, where there is a door. [As chap. 59 of the Rule suggests that the nuns did go into the basilica, an alternative translation for this passage would read ". . . never, up to the time of her death, go out of the monastery, nor (when) in the basilica, where there is seen to be a door" (Mother McCarthy's note).] . . .

Chapter 4. (Candidates must pass through a year's training under an elder religious before being admitted to community life and wearing of the habit)

She, therefore, who, by the inspiration of God undertakes religious life shall not be allowed immediately to assume the religious garb, until beforehand her will has been proved by many trials; but let her, in charge of one of the elder sisters, remain for a whole year in the garb in which she came. Moreover, concerning the matter of changing of garb, and of having a bed in the community dormitory, she shall be in the charge of this sister; and as the latter sees her character and her compunction, let her accordingly endeavor to mold her either rapidly or slowly.

Chapter 5. (Disposition of possessions of widows and married women who have left their husbands)

Those who come to the monastery as widows, or those who have left their husbands, or those who have changed their garb, cannot be received, unless beforehand they deed over, or give, or sell, to whomsoever they wish all their possessions, so that they reserve nothing in their own control which they govern or possess as private property, on account of the saying of the Lord: "If thou wilt be perfect, go sell what thou hast" (Matt. 19:21); and "If any one does not renounce all things and follow me, he cannot be my disciple" (Luke 14:26, 27, 33). This therefore I say to you, venerable daughters, because nuns who have possessions cannot have perfection. As to this matter, if they will not fulfill it, even those who have adopted religious life as virgins shall not be received, and certainly shall not be allowed to take the religious habit, until they rid themselves of all impediments of this world. . . .

Chapter 7. (Candidates must be at least six or seven years of age)

No one, not even the abbess, may be permitted to have her own maid for her service; but if they have need, let them receive help from the younger religious. And, if possible, never, or at best with difficulty, let little girls be received into the monastery, unless they are six or seven years old, so that they are able to learn their letters and to submit to obedience. The daughters either of nobility or of common folk are never to be received so that they may be reared or taught. . . .

Chapter 18. (Obedience to the abbess; reading customs)

All shall obey the mother after God; all should defer to the prioress. They shall be silent while sitting at the table and they shall direct their attention to the reading. Moreover, when the reading has ceased, holy meditation of the heart shall not cease. If there be some need, she who presides at table shall be solicitous and shall seek what is necessary by nod rather than by speech. Not only should the mouth take nourishment for you, but also let the ears hear the word of God. All shall learn to read. . . .

Chapter 71. (Regulations for food and drink)

It has seemed necessary to us to include even the procedure for meals in this Rule. On all days of fasting, three dishes are to be provided, but on days when lunch is taken, only two. On major feasts, at lunch and dinner dishes may be added, and iced wine mixed with [it] should be added for dessert. On ordinary days, at lunch in summer they are to receive two measures of hot drinks; in winter at lunch, two measures of hot drink; at the repast on fast days, three measures of hot drink; at dinner two measures of hot drink suffice. The younger sisters are to receive two at lunch, at dinner, and at the repast on fast days. Fowls are to be brought forth only for the sick; they are never to be served in community. No flesh meat is ever to be taken at all for nourishment; if, by chance, someone should be gravely ill, she may take it by the order and permission of the abbess.

Chapter 72. (Postscript one)

I beseech and supplicate you before our Lord God, O most dutiful sisters, in order for you to be perpetually grateful in this wise to my humble self and your holy mothers, that is, the founders of the monastery and the authors of the Rule; that you, by your charitable intercession keep watch for us day and night; and in public prayer through your holy supplication, obtain, in solemnities by day or vigils by night, that your petition, ascending in the sight of the Lord may make and grant me to be a worthy bishop over his Church, and them to be worthy superiors in the service of holy virgins; and when before His tribunal we begin to render an account of the talents entrusted to us, if there are faults and negligence, either concerning the care of my church, or of the mothers in regard to those committed to them, that the Lord will deign to pardon us, and to heal the wounds of sin with the medicine of forgiveness. For faults are not amended unless He remits them through the prayers of the saints, nor does He remit them unless they have been amended.

Chapter 73. (Postscript two)

And because for the sake of guarding the monastery, I have closed and forbidden the use of some doors, in the old baptistery, in the *scola* and in the weaving room, and in the tower next to the *pomerium*, let no one ever presume under any pretext of utility whatsoever to open them; but it shall be allowed to the holy congregation to offer resistance, and they are not to permit that to be done which they know to be against their good reputation or peace.

I, Caesarius, a sinner, have read and signed this rule for nuns. I have dated it under June 22, in the consulship of Paulinus (534).

I, Simplicius, a sinner, have approved and signed.

I, Severus, a bishop, have approved and signed.

I, Lupercianus, a bishop, have approved and signed.

I, John, have approved and signed.

I, Cyprianos, a bishop, have approved and signed.

I, Montanus, have approved and signed.

I, Firminus, a sinner, have approved and signed.

THE RULE OF THE MASTER

From *The Rule of the Master*, translated from the Latin by Luke Eberle; introduced by Adalbert de Vogüé and translated by Charles Philippi, pp. 118–24. Cistercian Studies 6. Kalamazoo, Mich.: Cistercian Publications, 1977.

The anonymous *Rule of the Master* was written around 500 by an unknown abbot and is generally accepted as the main source for the better known *Rule of Saint Benedict*, produced some forty years later. Benedict's greatest debt to the Master can be seen in the chapters on obedience, humility, and many organizational details. The following selection gives a sense of the Master's view regarding humility and obedience, taken up by Benedict almost verbatim in his Rule. The text makes use of the dialogue form to allow the Master his voice and authority, a form used by earlier monastic authorities.

Question of the disciples:
IV. What are the spiritual instruments which we can use to practice the divine art?
The Lord has replied through the master:
What are they? Faith, hope, charity (1 Cor. 13:13); peace, joy, mildness (Gal. 5:22–3); humility, obedience, silence; above all, chastity of the body; a sincere conscience; abstinence, purity, simplicity; kindness, goodness, compassion (Gal. 5:22); above all piety; temperance, vigilance, sobriety; justice, equity, truth; love, measure, moderation, and perseverance.

Question of the disciples:
V. What is the substance and cause of the evils which must be expurgated in the furnace of the fear of God,
And what is the rust and dirt of vices from which the abrasion of justice must cleanse us?
The Lord has replied through the master:

These are the vices which we must guard against: first of all, pride, then
disobedience, talkativeness; falsehood, avarice, cupidity; jealousy, envy,
iniquity; hatred, enmity, anger, quarreling, discord (Gal. 5:20); fornication, drunkenness, gluttony; murmuring, impiety, injustice, laziness,
theft; detraction, buffoonery, levity, impurity, idle speech; excessive or
guffawing laughter, humming; covetousness, deceit, ambition, insta-
bility. All these things are not from God but are the works of the devil
which on the day of judgment will get from God what they deserve,
the hell of everlasting fire (1 John 3:10, 8).

Question of the disciples:
VI. What is the workshop of the divine art and how are the spiritual
instruments used?
The Lord has replied through the master:
The workshop is the monastery (RB 5:1), where the instruments of
the heart are kept in the enclosure of the body, and the work of the
divine art can be accomplished with assiduous care and perseverance.

Question of the disciples:
VII. What should be the nature of the disciples' obedience?
The Lord has replied through the master:
The first degree of humility is obedience without delay. But this kind
is proper to the perfect, few in number, those who consider nothing more
dear to them than Christ; because of the holy service they have vowed,
for fear of hell, and for the sake of the treasures of eternal life, as soon
as they hear something commanded by the superior they can tolerate no
delay in conforming. It is of these that the Lord says: "No sooner do
they hear than they obey me" (Ps. 18:44). And he likewise says to those
who teach: "Anyone who listens to you listens to me" (Luke 10:16).
Such as these, therefore, immediately relinquishing their own concerns
and abandoning their own will, disengaging their hands and leaving unfinished what they were doing, comply by their actions with the voice
of the one who commands, falling into step with prompt obedience.
Thus in one and the same moment, so to speak, the command issued
by the superior and what is done by the disciples, the two together,
occur without any delay, in the swiftness of the fear of God.

But this kind of obedience, proper to the few who are perfect, should not unduly alarm the souls of the weak and the indolent and make them despair, but, should inspire them to do likewise. So keeping in mind that among us there are assorted embodiments of misery, since a sluggish nature is the source of a great deal of laziness in some persons—for it is well known that the hearing of certain ones is dulled by insensibility of the ears, and we also note that the minds of some are immediately distracted and wander off into a jungle of thoughts—we therefore indulgently moderate the strictures of obedience on the part of the teachers. Accordingly, the master should not be irked at having to repeat his command to the disciples, as the Lord testified when, calling Abraham, he repeated his name a second time, saying: "Abraham, Abraham" (Gen. 22:1). By this repetition the Lord clearly showed us that one call is possibly not enough to ensure (his) being heard.

As regards questions, when the master's voice is directed to the disciples, it is only right to indulge by a repetition of the question those who do not reply, in such a way that if the disciple remains silent at first he should not be held at fault, but it should be considered a mark of respect reserved for the master. In this reverence the virtuous disciple is credited with hesitating to break the silence he maintains in order not to overwhelm you with replies rushing from a glib tongue as soon as you state your question. But as regards commands, if the master must repeat his order, however slow or negligent the hearers may be, when what was first said is repeated to them a second time, it is by all means proper that the second delay be interrupted by acts of obedience. If however there should be a third delay on the disciple's part—may it never happen!—it must be considered a fault, the perversity of contumacy.

It is right and proper to consider here the theme of the two ways, namely, the broad road which leads to perdition, and the narrow road which leads to life (Matt. 7:13–14). On these two roads proceed the various types of human obedience. Thus, on the broad road go men of the world and sarabaite and gyrovague monks. These live alone or two or three together, without a superior, on an equal footing and moving about as they please. Alternating in authority, taking turns in commanding one another whatever each one wishes, safeguarding for themselves whatever they individually choose—since no one wants to be thwarted in his self-interest—such as these never banish dispute from themselves. Right after a violent quarrel these evilly-assembled men break up and wander off like a flock without a shepherd, dispersing in various directions, no doubt only to fall into the jaws of the wolf (cf. Matt. 9:36, Ezek. 34:5). It is not God who provides cells for them once again, but their self-will. Individually, on their own authority, each one for himself alone, they assume the title of abbot. And you find that there are more monasteries than monks.

One may be confident that such as these walk the broad road in that, while retaining the name monk, they live in the same way as do those in the world, distinguished from them only by having the tonsure. They give obedience to their desires instead of to God. Trusting their own judgment they think that what is evil is allowed to them; whatever they want they call holy, and whatever they do not want they consider forbidden. They deem it proper to think about providing for their body rather than for their soul, in other words, that they better than anyone else can be concerned about food, clothing, and footwear for themselves. They recklessly fancy themselves so secure as regards the account they will have to give of their soul that, whereas they are living as monks according to their own judgment without the guidance of superiors, they think that in their cell they are perfectly observant of every law and all the justice of God. If perchance some superior or other, in passing by, offers them some suggestions for their improvement and tells them that this solitary manner of living is not good for them, the advice as well as the very person of the teacher immediately displeases them. Unmoved, they do not promise to reform by agreeing with him and heeding him, but reply that they must live all alone, ignoring what the prophet said: "Such are corrupt; they do abominable deeds" (Ps. 14:1), and that testimony of Solomon which says: "There are ways which men think right, but whose end plunges into the depth of hell" (cf. Prov. 16:25).

Such as these therefore travel the broad way because wherever the foot of their desires leads them, they immediately consent to follow, and most willing indulgence is unhesitatingly at the service of whatever their lust craves (Passio 13). Breaking for themselves new paths of licentiousness and self-will without a master, they enlarge the way of their life by diverse kinds of forbidden pleasures, and toward whatever place their delights wish to go, they direct their wanton and criminal steps. They never want to realize that for the creature man, death is stationed at the entrance of delight (Passio 14), and they bypass with un-hearing ears what is said to them: "Do not follow your lusts; restrain your desires" (Sir. 18:30).

Those whom love urges on to eternal life, on the contrary, take the narrow way. Not living according to their own discretion or obeying their own desires and pleasures, but walking by the judgment and com-mand of another, they not only exercise self-control in the aforesaid desires and pleasures and do not want to do their own will even if they could, so but they also submit themselves to the authority of another. Living in monasteries, they wish to have an abbot over them and not bear this title themselves. Certainly such as these conform to what the Lord says: "I have come not to do my own will, but to do the will of the one who sent me" (John 6:38). And not doing their own will, deny-ing themselves for the sake of Christ, they follow God whithersoever the command of the abbot leads them.

Furthermore, under the care of the abbot, not only are they not forced to worry about temporal necessities, that is, food, clothing and footwear, but solely by rendering obedience in all things to the master, they are made secure about the account they will have to give of their soul and about whatever else is profitable for both body and soul. This is so because, whether for good or for ill, what happens among the sheep is the responsibility of the shepherd, and he who gave orders is the one who will have to render an account when inquiry is made at the judg-ment, not he who carried out the orders, whether good or bad.

Now, it may be said that such as these travel the narrow way, be-cause their own desires are never slightly put into effect and they do not do what they wish. But bearing the yoke of another's judgment, they are restrained from going where their own pleasure would lead them, and what they themselves would choose to do or achieve is denied them by the master. In the monastery their will is daily thwarted for the sake of the Lord, and in the spirit of martyrdom they patiently endure whatever commands they receive to test them. In the monas-tery they will assuredly say to the Lord, with the prophet: "For your sake we are being slain all the day; we are looked upon as sheep to be slaughtered" (Ps. 44:22). And later on, at the judgment, they will likewise say to the lord: "You tested us, God, you refined us like silver. You let us fall into the net. You laid heavy burdens on our backs. You have set men over our heads" (Ps. 66:10–12). Therefore when they say, "You have set men over our heads," it is evident that they are to have over them as God's representative a superior, whom they fear in the monastery. And continuing with what is stated, they will rightly say to the Lord again, this time in the next world: "But now the ordeal by fire and water is over, and you allow us once more to draw breath" (Ps. 66:12), that is, "We have gone through the thwarting of our own will and by serving in obedience we have come to the enjoyment of your love."

But obedience such as this will be acceptable to God and gratifying to men only if the thing commanded is done without fear, without apathy, without hesitation, without murmuring or protesting, because obedience offered to superiors is given to God, as the Lord says to our teachers: "Anyone who listens to you listens to me" (Luke 10:16), and elsewhere he says: "No sooner do they hear than they obey me" (Ps. 18:44). Obedience is such, therefore, if it is given with good will, because "God loves a cheerful giver" (2 Cor. 9:7). The disciple obeys with ill will if he reproaches not only us verbally but God inwardly about what he does in a bad mood. And even though he does what he was commanded, still it will not be acceptable to God, who sees that he is murmuring in his heart. To repeat, even though he does what he is told, but does it in a bad mood, he will get no reward for doing it, for God is watching his heart right now and finds in it the wretched disposition of one who acts in this way.

THE RULE OF ST. BENEDICT

From *The Rule of St. Benedict*, edited by Timothy Fry, O.S.B., Imogene Baker, O.S.B., Timothy Horner, O.S.B., Augusta Baabe, O.S.B., and Mark Sheridan, O.S.B. Collegeville, Minn.: The Liturgical Press, 1982.

This is the *Rule of Saint Benedict*, authored by Benedict of Nursia, around 535. Benedict is also known especially for founding the monastery at Monte Casino, Italy. Central to Benedict's Rule is the *Opus dei*, the work of God, which dominates the daily monastic routine, regulating seven times a day for communal prayer. Benedict legislates that *lectio divina* ought to play a central role in the lives of his followers, while manual labor should occupy the balance of the day. The monk was required to take three vows: *conversio morum*, which refers to the conversion of life-style of a particular community; the vow of *stabilitas loci*, a vow to remain a member of a specific community; and, *obediencia*, obedience to the abbot, clearly established by Benedict as Vicar of Christ and spiritual father to the entire community. Other images of the abbot in the Rule established that he was to act as a teacher, shepherd, and doctor. Note the centrality of the virtue of humility and importance of obedience, often seen as reflecting the words of the earlier and longer *Rule of the Master*. Later, it was mandated by Louis the Pious, emperor son of Charlemagne, as the Rule for the Empire and becomes the dominant Rule in the West.

Prologue

Listen carefully, my son, to the master's instructions, and attend to them with the ear of your heart. This is advice from a father who loves you; welcome it, and faithfully put it into practice. The labor of obedience will bring you back to him from whom you had drifted through the sloth of disobedience. This message of mine is for you, then, if you are ready to give up your own will, once and for all, and armed with the strong and noble weapons of obedience to do battle for the true King, Christ the Lord.

First of all, every time you begin a good work, you must pray to him most earnestly to bring it to perfection. In his goodness, he has already counted us as his sons, and therefore we should never grieve him by our evil actions. With his good gifts which are in us, we must obey him at all times that he may never become the angry father who disinherits his sons, nor the dread lord, enraged by our sins, who punishes us forever as worthless servants for refusing to follow him to glory.

Let us get up then, at long last, for the Scriptures rouse us when they say: *It is high time for us to arise from sleep* (Rom. 13:11). Let us open our eyes to the light that comes from God, and our ears to the voice from heaven that every day calls out this charge: *If you hear his voice today, do not harden your hearts* (Ps. 94:8). And again: *You that have ears to hear, listen to what the Spirit says to the churches* (Rev. 2:7). And what does he say? *Come and listen to me, sons; I will teach you the fear of the Lord* (Ps. 33:12). *Run while you have the light* of life, *that the darkness* of death *may not overtake you* (John 12:35).

Seeking his workman in a multitude of people, the Lord calls out to him and lifts his voice again: *Is there anyone here who yearns for life and desires to see good days?* (Ps. 33:13). If you hear this and your answer is "I do," God then directs these words to you: If you desire true and eternal life, *keep your tongue free from vicious talk and your lips from all deceit; turn away from evil and do good; let peace be your quest and aim* (Ps. 33:14–15). Once you have done this, my *eyes will be upon* you *and* my *ears will listen* for your *prayers; and even before you ask me, I will say* to you: *Here I am* (Isa. 58:9). What, dear brothers, is more delightful than this voice of the Lord calling to us? See how the Lord in his love shows us the way of life. Clothed then with faith and the performance of good works, let us set out on this way, with the Gospel for our guide, that we may deserve to see him *who has called* us *to his kingdom* (1 Thess. 2:12).

If we wish to dwell in the tent of this kingdom, we will never arrive unless we run there by doing good deeds. But let us ask the Lord with the Prophet; *Who will dwell in your tent, Lord; who will find rest upon your holy mountain?* (Ps. 14:1). After this question, brothers, let us listen well to what the Lord says in reply, for he shows us the way to his tent. *One who walks without blemish,* he says, *and is just in all his dealings; who speaks the truth from his heart and has not practiced deceit with his tongue; who has not wronged a fellow man in any way, nor listened to slanders against his neighbor* (Ps. 14:2–3). He has *foiled* the *evil one*, the devil, at every turn, flinging both him and his promptings far *from the sight* of his heart. While these temptations were still *young, he caught hold of them and dashed them against* Christ (Ps. 14:4; 136:9). These people *fear the Lord,* and do not become elated over their good deeds; they judge it is the Lord's power, not their own, that brings about the good in them. *They praise* (Ps. 14:4) the Lord working in them, and say with the Prophet: *Not to us, Lord, not to us give the glory, but to your name alone* (Ps. 113:9). In just this way Paul the Apostle refused to take credit for the power of his preaching. He declared: *By God's grace I am what I am* (1 Cor. 15:10). And again he said: *He who boasts should make his boast in the Lord* (2 Cor. 10:17). That is why the Lord says in the Gospel: *Whoever hears these words of mine and does them is like a wise man who built his house upon rock; the floods came and the winds blew and beat against the house, but it did not fall: it was founded on rock* (Matt. 7:24–25).

With this conclusion, the Lord waits for us daily to translate into action, as we should, his holy teachings. Therefore our life span has been lengthened by way of a truce, that we may amend our misdeeds. As the Apostle says: *Do you not know that the patience of God is leading you to repent?* (Rom. 2:4). And indeed the Lord assures us in his love: *I do not wish the death of the sinner, but that he turn back to me and live* (Ezek. 33:11).

Brothers, now that we have asked the Lord who will dwell in his tent, we have heard the instruction for dwelling in it, but only if we fulfill the obligations of those who live there. We must, then, prepare our hearts and bodies for the battle of holy obedience to his instructtions. What is not possible to us by nature, let us ask the Lord to supply by the help of his grace. If we wish to reach eternal life, even as we avoid the torments of hell, then—while there is still time, while we are in this body and have time to accomplish all these things by the light of life—we must run and do now what will profit us forever.

Therefore we intend to establish a school for the Lord's service. In drawing up its regulations, we hope to set down nothing harsh, nothing burdensome. The good of all concerned, however, may prompt us to a little strictness in order to amend faults and to safeguard love. Do not be daunted immediately by fear and run away from the road that leads to salvation. It is bound to be narrow at the outset. But as we progress in this way of life and in faith, we shall run on the path of God's commandments, our hearts overflowing with the inexpressible delight of love. Never swerving from his instructions, then, but faithfully observing his teaching in the monastery until death, we shall through patience share in the sufferings of Christ that we may deserve also to share in his kingdom. Amen.

Chapter 2. Qualities of the Abbot

To be worthy of the task of governing a monastery, the abbot must always remember what his title signifies and act as a superior should. He is believed to hold the place of Christ in the monastery, since he is addressed by a title of Christ, as the Apostle indicates: *You have received the spirit of adoption of sons by which we exclaim, abba, father* (Rom. 8:15). Therefore, the abbot must never teach or decree or command anything that would deviate from the Lord's instructions. On the contrary, everything he teaches and commands should, like the leaven of divine justice, permeate the minds of his disciples. Let the abbot always remember that at the fearful judgment of God, not only his teaching but also his disciples' obedience will come under scrutiny. The abbot must, therefore, be aware that the shepherd will bear the blame wherever the father of the household finds that the sheep have yielded no profit. Still, if he has faithfully shepherded a restive and disobedient flock, always striving to cure their unhealthy ways, it will be otherwise: the shepherd will be acquitted at the Lord's judgment. Then, like the Prophet, he may say to the Lord: *I have not hidden your justice in my heart; I have proclaimed your truth and your salvation* (Ps. 39:11), *but they spurned and rejected me* (Isa. 1:2; Ezek. 20:27). Then at last the sheep that have rebelled against his care will be punished by the overwhelming power of death.

Furthermore, anyone who receives the name of abbot is to lead his disciples by a twofold teaching: he must point out to them all that is good and holy more by example than by words, proposing the commandments of the Lord to receptive disciples with words, but demonstrating God's instructions to the stubborn and the dull by a living example. Again, if he teaches his disciples that something is not to be done, then neither must he do it, *lest after preaching to others, he himself be found reprobate* (1 Cor. 9:27) and God some day call to him in his sin: *How is it that you repeat my just commands and mouth my covenant when you hate discipline and toss my words behind you?* (Ps. 49:16–17). And also this: *How is it that you can see a splinter in your brother's eye, and never notice the plank in your own?* (Matt. 7:3). The abbot should avoid all favoritism in the monastery. He is not to love one more than another unless he finds someone better in good actions and obedience. A man born free is not to be given higher rank than a slave who becomes a monk, except for some other good reason. But the abbot is free, if he sees fit, to change anyone's rank as justice demands. Ordinarily, everyone is to keep to his regular place, because *whether slave or free, we are all one in Christ* (Gal. 3:28; Eph. 6:8) and share alike in bearing arms in the service of the one Lord, for *God shows no partiality among persons* (Rom. 2:11). Only in this are we distinguished in his sight: if we are found better than others in good works and in humility. Therefore, the abbot is to show equal love to everyone and apply the same discipline to all according to their merits.

In his teaching, the abbot should always observe the Apostle's recommendation, in which he says: *Use argument, appeal, reproof* (2 Tim. 4:2). This means that he must vary with circumstances, threatening and coaxing by turns, stern as a taskmaster, devoted and tender as only a father can be. With the undisciplined and restless, he will use firm argument; with the obedient and docile and patient, he will appeal for greater virtue; but as for the negligent and disdainful, we charge him to use reproof and rebuke. He should not gloss over the sins of those who err, but cut them out while he can, as soon as they begin to sprout, remembering the fate of Eli, priest of Shiloh (1 Sam. 2:11–4:18). For upright and perceptive men, his first and second warnings should be verbal; but those who are evil or stubborn, arrogant or disobedient, he can curb only by blows or some other physical punishment at the first offense. It is written, *The fool cannot be corrected with words* (Prov. 29:19); and again, *Strike your son with a rod and you will free his soul from death* (Prov. 23:14).

The abbot must always remember what he is and remember what he is called, aware that more will be expected of a man to whom more has been entrusted. He must know what a difficult and demanding burden he has undertaken: directing souls and serving a variety of temperaments, coaxing, reproving and encouraging them as appropriate. He must so accommodate and adapt himself to each one's character and intelligence that he will not only keep the flock entrusted to his care from dwindling, but will rejoice in the increase of a good flock. Above all, he must not show too great concern for the fleeting and temporal things of this world, neglecting or treating lightly the welfare of those entrusted to him. Rather, he should keep in mind that he has undertaken the care of souls for whom he must give an account. That he may not plead lack of resources as an excuse, he is to remember what is written: *Seek first the kingdom of God and his justice, and all these things will be given you as well* (Matt. 6:33), and again, *Those who fear him lack nothing* (Ps. 33:10).

The abbot must know that anyone undertaking the charge of souls must be ready to account for them. Whatever the number of brothers he has in his care, let him realize that on judgment day he will surely have to submit a reckoning to the Lord for all their souls—and indeed for his own as well. In this way, while always fearful of the future examination of the shepherd about the sheep entrusted to him and careful about the state of others' accounts, he becomes concerned also about his own, and while helping others to amend by his warnings, he achieves the amendment of his own faults.

Chapter 3. Summoning the Brothers for Counsel

As often as anything important is to be done in the monastery, the abbot shall call the whole community together and himself explain what the business is; and after hearing the advice of the brothers, let him ponder it and follow what he judges the wiser course. The reason why we have said all should be called for counsel is that the Lord often reveals what is better to the younger. The brothers, for their part, are to express their opinions with all humility, and not presume to defend their own views obstinately. The decision is rather the abbot's to make, so that when he has determined what is more prudent, all may obey. Nevertheless, just as it is proper for disciples to obey their master, so it is becoming for the master on his part to settle everything with foresight and fairness.

Accordingly in every instance, all are to follow the teaching of the rule, and no one shall rashly deviate from it. In the monastery no one is to follow his own heart's desire, nor shall anyone presume to contend with his abbot defiantly, or outside the monastery. Should anyone presume to do so, let him be subjected to the discipline of the rule. Moreover, the abbot himself must fear God and keep the rule in everything he does; he can be sure beyond any doubt that he will have to give an account of all his judgments to God, the most just of judges.

If less important business of the monastery is to be transacted, he shall take counsel with the seniors only, as it is written: *Do everything with counsel and you will not be sorry afterward* (Sir. 32:24).

Chapter 4. The Tools for Good Works

First of all, *love the Lord God with your whole heart, your whole soul and all your strength, and love your neighbor as yourself* (Matt. 22:37–39; Mark 12:30–31; Luke 10:27). Then the following: *You are not to kill, you are not to commit adultery; you are not to steal nor to covet* (Rom. 13:9), *you are not to bear false witness* (Matt. 19:18; Mark 10:19; Luke 18:20). *You must honor everyone* (1 Pet. 2:17), and *never do to another what you do not want done to yourself* (Tob. 4:16; Matt. 7:12; Luke 6:31).

Renounce yourself in order to follow Christ (Matt. 16:24; Luke 9:23); *discipline your body* (1 Cor. 9:27); do not pamper yourself, but love fasting. You must relieve the lot of the poor, *clothe the naked, visit the sick* (Matt. 25:36), and bury the dead. Go to help the troubled and console the sorrowing.

Your way of acting should be different from the world's way; the love of Christ must come before all else. You are not to act in anger or nurse a grudge. Rid your heart of all deceit. Never give a hollow greeting of peace or turn away when someone needs your love. Bind yourself to no oath lest it prove false, but speak the truth with heart and tongue.

Do not repay one bad turn with another (1 Thess. 5:15; 1 Pet. 3:9). Do not injure anyone, but bear injuries patiently. *Love your enemies* (Matt. 5:44; Luke 6:27). If people curse you, do not curse them back but bless them instead. *Endure persecution for the sake of justice* (Matt. 5:10).

You must *not* be *proud, nor be given to wine* (Titus 1:7; 1 Tim. 3:3). Refrain from too much eating or sleeping, and *from laziness* (Rom. 12:11). Do not grumble or speak ill of others.

Place your hope in God alone. If you notice something good in yourself, give credit to God, not to yourself, but be certain that the evil you commit is always your own and yours to acknowledge.

Live in fear of judgment day and have a great horror of hell. Yearn for everlasting life with holy desire. Day by day remind yourself that you are going to die. Hour by hour keep careful watch over all you do, aware that God's gaze is upon you, wherever you may be. As soon as wrongful thoughts come into your heart, dash them against Christ and disclose them to your spiritual father. Guard your lips from harmful or deceptive speech. Prefer moderation in speech and speak no foolish chatter, nothing just to provoke laughter; do not love immoderate or boisterous laughter.

Listen readily to holy reading, and devote yourself often to prayer. Every day with tears and sighs confess your past sins to God in prayer and change from these evil ways in the future.

Do not gratify the promptings of the flesh (Gal. 5:16); hate the urgings of self-will. Obey the orders of the abbot unreservedly, even if his own conduct—which God forbid—be at odds with what he says. Remember the teaching of the Lord: *Do what they say, not what they do* (Matt. 23:3).

Do not aspire to be called holy before you really are, but first be holy that you may more truly be called so. Live by God's command-ments every day; treasure chastity, harbor neither hatred nor jealousy of anyone, and do nothing out of envy. Do not love quarreling; shun arrogance. Respect the elders and love the young. Pray for your enemies out of love for Christ. If you have a dispute with someone, make peace with him before the sun goes down.

And finally, never lose hope in God's mercy.

These, then, are the tools of the spiritual craft. When we have used them without ceasing day and night and have returned them on judgment day, our wages will be the reward the Lord has promised: *What the eye has not seen nor the ear heard, God has prepared for those who love him* (1 Cor. 2:9). The workshop where we are to toil faithfully at all these tasks is the enclosure of the monastery and stability in the community.

Chapter 5. Obedience

The first step of humility is unhesitating obedience, which comes naturally to those who cherish Christ above all. Because of the holy service they have professed, or because of dread of hell and for the glory of everlasting life, they carry out the superior's order as promptly as if the command came from God himself. The Lord says of men like this: *No sooner did he hear than he obeyed me* (Ps. 17:45); again, he tells teachers: *Whoever listens to you, listens to me* (Luke 10:16). Such people as these immediately put aside their own concerns, abandon their own will, and lay down whatever they have in hand, leaving it unfinished. With the ready step of obedience, they follow the voice of authority in their actions. Almost at the same moment, then, as the master gives the instruction the disciple quickly puts it into practice in the fear of God; and both actions together are swiftly completed as one.

It is love that impels them to pursue everlasting life; therefore, they are eager to take the narrow road of which the Lord says: *Narrow is the road that leads to life* (Matt. 7:14). They no longer live by their own judgment, giving in to their whims and appetites; rather they walk according to another's decisions and directions, choosing to live in monasteries and to have an abbot over them. Men of this resolve unquestionably conform to the saying of the Lord: *I have come not to do my own will, but the will of him who sent me* (John 6:38).

This very obedience, however, will be acceptable to God and agreeable to men only if compliance with what is commanded is not cringing or sluggish or half-hearted, but free from any grumbling or any reaction of unwillingness. For the obedience shown to superiors is given to God, as he himself said: *Whoever listens to you, listens to me* (Luke 10:16). Furthermore, the disciples' obedience must be given gladly, for *God loves a cheerful giver* (2 Cor. 9:7). If a disciple obeys grudgingly and grumbles, not only aloud but also in his heart, then, even though he carries out the order, his action will not be accepted with favor by God, who sees that he is grumbling in his heart. He will have no reward for service of this kind; on the contrary, he will incur punishment for grumbling, unless he changes for the better and makes amends.

Chapter 7. Humility

Brothers, divine Scripture calls to us saying: *Whoever exalts himself shall be humbled, and whoever humbles himself shall be exalted* (Luke 14:11; 18:14). In saying this, therefore, it shows us that every exaltation is a kind of pride, which the Prophet indicates he has shunned, saying: *Lord, my heart is not exalted; my eyes are not lifted up and I have not walked in the ways of the great nor gone after marvels beyond me* (Ps. 130:1). And why? *If I had not a humble spirit, but were exalted instead, then you would treat me like a weaned child on its mother's lap* (Ps. 130:2).

Accordingly, brothers, if we want to reach the highest summit of humility, if we desire to attain speedily that exaltation in heaven to which we climb by the humility of this present life, then by our ascending actions we must set up that ladder on which Jacob in a dream saw *angels descending and ascending* (Gen. 28:12). Without doubt, this descent and ascent can signify only that we descend by exaltation and ascend by humility. Now the ladder erected is our life on earth, and if we humble our hearts the Lord will raise it to heaven. We may call our body and soul the sides of this ladder, into which our divine vocation has fitted the various steps of humility and discipline as we ascend.

The first step of humility, then, is that a man keeps the *fear of God* always *before his eyes* (Ps. 35:2) and never forgets it. He must constantly remember everything God has commanded, keeping in mind that all who despise God will burn in hell for their sins, and all who fear God have everlasting life awaiting them. While he guards himself at every moment from sins and vices of thought or tongue, of hand or foot, of self-will or bodily desire, let him recall that he is always seen by God in heaven, that his actions everywhere are in God's sight and are reported by angels at every hour.

The Prophet indicates this to us when he shows that our thoughts are always present to God, saying: *God searches hearts and minds* (Ps. 7:10); again he says: *The Lord knows the thoughts of men* (Ps. 93:11); likewise, *From afar you know my thoughts* (Ps. 138:2); and, *The thoughts of man shall give you praise* (Ps. 75:11). That he may take care to avoid sinful thoughts, the virtuous brother must always say to himself: *I shall be blameless in his sight* if *I guard myself from my own wickedness* (Ps. 17:24).

Truly, we are forbidden to do our own will, for Scripture tells us: *Turn away from your desires* (Sir. 18:30). And in the Prayer too we ask God that his *will be done* in us (Matt. 6:10). We are rightly taught not to do our own will, since we dread what Scripture says: *There are ways which men call right that in the end plunge into the depths of hell* (Prov. 16:25). Moreover, we fear what is said of those who ignore this: *They are corrupt and have become depraved in their desires* (Ps. 13:1).

As for the desires of the body, we must believe that God is always with us, for *All my desires are known to you* (Ps. 37:10), as the Prophet tells the Lord. We must then be on guard against any base desire, because death is stationed near the gateway of pleasure. For this reason Scripture warns us, *Pursue not your lusts* (Sir. 18:30).

Accordingly, if *the eyes of the Lord are watching the good and the wicked* (Prov. 15:3), *if at all times the Lord looks down from heaven on the sons of men to see whether any understand and seek God* (Ps. 13:2); and if every day the angels assigned to us report our deeds to the Lord day and night, then, brothers, we must be vigilant every hour or, as the Prophet says in the psalm, God may observe us *falling* at some time into evil and *so made worthless* (Ps. 13:3). After sparing us for a while because he is a loving father who waits for us to improve, he may tell us later, *This you did, and I said nothing* (Ps. 49:21).

The second step of humility is that a man loves not his own will nor takes pleasure in the satisfaction of his desires; rather he shall imitate by his actions that saying of the Lord: *I have come not to do my own will, but the will of him who sent me* (John 6:38). Similarly we read, "Consent merits punishment; constraint wins a crown."

The third step of humility is that a man submits to his superior in all obedience for the love of God, imitating the Lord of whom the Apostle says: *He became obedient even to death* (Phil. 2:8).

The fourth step of humility is that in this obedience under difficult, unfavorable, or even unjust conditions, his heart quietly embraces suffering and endures it without weakening or seeking escape. For Scripture has it: *Anyone who perseveres to the end will be saved* (Matt. 10:22), and again, *Be brave of heart and rely on the Lord* (Ps. 26:14). Another passage shows how the faithful must endure everything, even contradiction, for the Lord's sake, saying in the person of those who suffer, *For your sake we are put to death continually; we are regarded as sheep marked for slaughter* (Rom. 8:36; Ps. 43:22). They are so confident in their expectation of reward from God that they continue joyfully and say, *But in all this we overcome because of him who so greatly loved us* (Rom. 8:37). Elsewhere Scripture says: *O God, you have tested us, you have tried us as silver is tried by fire; you have led us into a snare, you have placed afflicttions on our backs* (Ps. 65:10–11). Then, to show that we ought to be under a superior, it adds: *You have placed men over our heads* (Ps. 65:12).

In truth, those who are patient amid hardships and unjust treatment are fulfilling the Lord's command: *When struck on one cheek, they turn the other; when deprived of their coat, they offer their cloak also; when pressed into service for one mile, they go two* (Matt. 5:39–41). With the Apostle Paul, they bear with *false brothers, endure persecution*, and *bless those who curse them* (2 Cor. 11:26; 1 Cor. 4:12).

The fifth step of humility is that a man does not conceal from his abbot any sinful thoughts entering his heart, or any wrongs committed in secret, but rather confesses them humbly. Concerning this, Scripture exhorts us: *Make known your way to the Lord and hope in him* (Ps. 36:5). And again, *Confess to the Lord, for he is good; his mercy is forever* (Ps. 105:1; Ps. 117:1). So too the Prophet: *To you I have acknowledged my offense; my faults I have not concealed. I have said: Against myself I will report my faults to the Lord, and you have forgiven the wickedness of my heart* (Ps. 31:5).

The sixth step of humility is that a monk is content with the lowest and most menial treatment, and regards himself as a poor and worthless workman in whatever task he is given, saying to himself with the Prophet: *I am insignificant and ignorant, no better than a beast before you, yet I am with you always* (Ps. 72:22–23).

The seventh step of humility is that a man not only admits with his tongue but is also convinced in his heart that he is inferior to all and of less value, humbling himself and saying with the Prophet: *I am truly a worm, not a man, scorned by men and despised by the people* (Ps. 21:7). *I was exalted, then I was humbled and overwhelmed with confusion* (Ps. 87:16). And again, *It is a blessing that you have humbled me so that I can learn your commandments* (Ps. 118:71, 73).

The eighth step of humility is that a monk does only what is endorsed by the common rule of the monastery and the example set by his superiors.

The ninth step of humility is that a monk controls his tongue and remains silent, not speaking unless asked a question, for Scripture warns, *In a flood of words you will not avoid sinning* (Prov. 10:19), and, *A talkative man goes about aimlessly on earth* (Ps. 139:12).

The tenth step of humility is that he is not given to ready laughter, for it is written: *Only a fool raises his voice in laughter* (Sir. 21:23).

The eleventh step of humility is that a monk speaks gently and without laughter, seriously and with becoming modesty, briefly and reasonably, but without raising his voice, as it is written: "A wise man is known by his few words."

The twelfth step of humility is that a monk always manifests humility in his bearing no less than in his heart, so that it is evident at the Work of God (*Opus Dei*), in the oratory, the monastery or the garden, on a journey or in the field, or anywhere else. Whether he sits, walks or stands, his head must be bowed and his eyes cast down. Judging himself always guilty on account of his sins, he should consider that he is already at the fearful judgment, and constantly say in his heart what the publican in the Gospel said with downcast eyes: *Lord, I am a sinner, not worthy to look up to heaven* (Luke 18:13). And with the Prophet: *I am bowed down and humbled in every way* (Ps. 37:7–9; Ps. 118:107).

Now, therefore, after ascending all these steps of humility, the monk will quickly arrive at that *perfect love* of God which *casts out fear* (1 John 4:18). Through this love, all that he once performed with dread, he will now begin to observe without effort, as though naturally, from habit, no longer out of fear of hell, but out of love for Christ, good habit and delight in virtue. All this the Lord will by the Holy Spirit graciously manifest in his workman now cleansed of vices and sins.

Chapter 39. The Proper Amount of Food

For the daily meals, whether at noon or in mid-afternoon, it is enough, we believe, to provide all tables with two kinds of cooked food because of individual weaknesses. In this way, the person who may not be able to eat one kind of food may partake of the other. Two kinds of cooked food, therefore, should suffice for all the brothers, and if fruit or fresh vegetables are available, a third dish may also be added. A generous pound of bread is enough for a day whether for only one meal or for both dinner and supper. In the latter case the cellarer will set aside one third of this pound and give it to the brothers at supper.

Should it happen that the work is heavier than usual, the abbot may decide—and he will have the authority—to grant something additional, provided that it is appropriate, and that above all overindulgence is avoided, lest a monk experience indigestion. For nothing is so inconsistent with the life of any Christian as overindulgence. Our Lord says: *Take care that your hearts are not weighed down with overindulgence* (Luke 21:34).

Young boys should not receive the same amount as their elders, but less, since in all matters frugality is the rule. Let everyone, except the sick who are very weak, abstain entirely from eating the meat of four-footed animals.

Chapter 40. The Proper Amount of Drink

Everyone has his own gift from God, one this and another that (1 Cor. 7:7). It is, therefore, with some uneasiness that we specify the amount of food and drink for others. However, with due regard for the infirmities of the sick, we believe that a half bottle of wine a day is sufficient for each. But those to whom God gives the strength to abstain must know that they will earn their own reward.

The superior will determine when local conditions, work or the summer heat indicates the need for a greater amount. He must, in any case, take great care lest excess or drunkenness creep in. We read that monks should not drink wine at all, but since the monks of our day cannot be convinced of this, let us at least agree to drink moderately, and not to the point of excess, for *wine makes even wise men go astray* (Sir. 19:2).

However, where local circumstances dictate an amount much less than what is stipulated above, or even none at all, those who live there should bless God and not grumble. Above all else we admonish them to refrain from grumbling.

Chapter 48. The Daily Manual Labor

Idleness is the enemy of the soul. Therefore, the brothers should have specified periods for manual labor as well as for prayerful reading.

We believe that the times for both may be arranged as follows: From Easter to the first of October, they will spend their mornings after Prime till about the fourth hour at whatever work needs to be done. From the fourth hour until the time of Sext, they will devote themselves to reading. But after Sext and their meal, they may rest on their beds in complete silence; should a brother wish to read privately, let him do so, but without disturbing the others. They should say None a little early, about midway through the eighth hour, and then until Vespers they are to return to whatever work is necessary. They must not become distressed if local conditions or their poverty should force them to do the harvesting themselves. When they live by the labor of their hands, as our fathers and the apostles did, then they are really monks. Yet, all things are to be done with moderation on account of the fainthearted.

From the first of October to the beginning of Lent, the brothers ought to devote themselves to reading until the end of the second hour. At this time Terce is said and they are to work at their assigned tasks until None. At the first signal for the hour of None, all put aside their work to be ready for the second signal. Then after their meal they will devote themselves to their reading or to the psalms.

During the days of Lent, they should be free in the morning to read until the third hour, after which they will work at their assigned tasks until the end of the tenth hour. During this time of Lent each one is to receive a book from the library, and is to read the whole of it straight through. These books are to be distributed at the beginning of Lent.

Above all, one or two seniors must surely be deputed to make the rounds of the monastery while the brothers are reading. Their duty is to see that no brother is so apathetic as to waste time or engage in idle talk to the neglect of his reading, and so not only harm himself but also distract others. If such a monk is found—God forbid—he should be reproved a first and a second time. If he does not amend, he must be subjected to the punishment of the rule as a warning to others. Further, brothers ought not to associate with one another at inappropriate times.

On Sunday all are to be engaged in reading except those who have been assigned various duties. If anyone is so remiss and indolent that he is unwilling or unable to study or to read, he is to be given some work in order that he may not be idle. Brothers who are sick or weak should be given a type of work or craft that will keep them busy without overwhelming them or driving them away. The abbot must take their infirmities into account.

Chapter 58. The Procedure for Receiving Brothers

Do not grant newcomers to the monastic life an easy entry, but, as the Apostle says, *Test the spirits to see if they are from God* (1 John 4:1). Therefore, if someone comes and keeps knocking at the door, and if at the end of four or five days he has shown himself patient in bearing his harsh treatment and difficulty of entry, and has persisted in his request, then he should be allowed to enter and stay in the guest quarters for a few days. After that, he should live in the novitiate, where the novices study, eat and sleep.

A senior chosen for his skill in winning souls should be appointed to look after them with careful attention. The concern must be whether the novice truly seeks God and whether he shows eagerness for the Work of God, for obedience and for trials. The novice should be clearly told all the hardships and difficulties that will lead him to God.

If he promises perseverance in his stability, then after two months have elapsed let this Rule be read straight through to him, and let him be told: "This is the law under which you are choosing to serve. If you can keep it, come in. If not, feel free to leave." If he still stands firm, he is to be taken back to the novitiate, and again thoroughly tested in patience. After six months have passed, the Rule is to be read to him, so that he may know what he is entering. If once more he stands firm, let four months go by, and then read this Rule to him again. If after due reflection he promises to observe everything and to obey every command given him, let him then be received into the community. But he must be well aware that, as the law of the Rule establishes, from this day he is no longer free to leave the monastery, nor to shake from his neck the yoke of the Rule which, in the course of so prolonged a period of reflection, he was free either to reject or to accept.

When he is to be received, he comes before the whole community in the oratory and promises stability, fidelity to monastic life, and obedience. This is done in the presence of God and his saints to impress on the novice that if he ever acts otherwise, he will surely be condemned by the one he mocks. He states his promise in a document drawn up in the name of the saints whose relics are there, and of the abbot, who is present. The novice writes out this document himself, or if he is illiterate, then he asks someone else to write it for him, but himself puts his mark to it and with his own hand lays it on the altar. After he has put it there, the novice himself begins the verse: *Receive me*, Lord, *as you have promised, and I shall live; do not disappoint me in my hope* (Ps. 118:116). The whole community repeats the verse three times, and adds "Glory be to the Father." Then the novice prostrates himself at the feet of each monk to ask his prayers, and from that very day he is to be counted as one of the community.

If he has any possessions, he should either give them to the poor beforehand, or make a formal donation of them to the monastery, without keeping back a single thing for himself, well aware that from that day he will not have even his own body at his disposal. Then and there in the oratory, he is to be stripped of everything of his own that he is wearing and clothed in what belongs to the monastery. The clothing taken from him is to be put away and kept safely in the wardrobe, so that, should he ever agree to the devil's suggestion and leave the monastery—which God forbid—he can be stripped of the clothing of the monastery before he is cast out. But that document of his which the abbot took from the altar should not be given back to him but kept in the monastery.

Chapter 72. The Good Zeal of Monks

Just as there is a wicked zeal of bitterness which separates from God and leads to hell, so there is a good zeal which separates from evil and leads to God and everlasting life. This, then, is the good zeal which monks must foster with fervent love: *They should each try to be the first to show respect to the other* (Rom. 12:10), supporting with the greatest patience one another's weaknesses of body or behavior, and earnestly competing in obedience to one another. No one is to pursue what he judges better for himself, but instead, what he judges better for someone else. To their fellow monks they show the pure love of brothers; to God, loving fear; to their abbot, unfeigned and humble love. Let them prefer nothing whatever to Christ, and may he bring us all together to everlasting life.

Chapter 73. This Rule Only a Beginning of Perfection

The reason we have written this Rule is that, by observing it in monasteries, we can show that we have some degree of virtue and the beginnings of monastic life. But for anyone hastening on to the perfection of monastic life, there are the teachings of the holy Fathers, the observance of which will lead him to the very heights of perfection. What page, what passage of the inspired books of the Old and New Testaments is not the truest of guides for human life? What book of the holy catholic Fathers does not resoundingly summon us along the true way to reach the Creator? Then, besides the *Conferences* of the Fathers, their *Institutes* and their *Lives*, there is also the rule of our holy father Basil. For observant and obedient monks, all these are nothing less than tools for the cultivation of virtues; but as for us, they make us blush for shame at being so slothful, so unobservant, so negligent. Are you hastening toward your heavenly home? Then with Christ's help, keep this little Rule that we have written for beginners. After that, you can set out for the loftier summits of the teaching and virtues we mentioned above, and under God's protection you will reach them. Amen.

RULE FOR MONKS BY COLUMBANUS

From *Sancti Columbani Opera*, edited by G. S. M. Walker. Shannon, Ireland: The Dublin Institute for Advanced Studies, Irish University Press, 1957; reprinted 1970.

Columbanus was born in West Leinster, Ireland, in 543, and died at Bobbio, Italy, in 615. Columbanus entered the monastic life at the famous monastery of Bangor and remained there several years before receiving permission to evangelize on the continent. It is assumed that in 591, Columbanus and several monks from Bangor established Celtic monasticism in Western Europe, founding monasteries in France at Annegray and Luxeuil, and later Bobbio, in Italy. These communities grew quickly and became large enough to benefit from a written Rule. Columbanus' Rule dates from around the mid- to late 590s. This Celtic Rule displays little of the flexibility of the Rule of Benedict and scholars often remark on the severity of its austerity. This selection includes a section on the discipline found in a Celtic monastery.

Here begins the Monks' Rule of St. Columban
First of all things we are taught: to love God with the whole heart and the whole mind and all our strength, and our neighbor as ourselves; next, our works.

I. Of Obedience

At the first word of a senior, all on hearing should rise to obey, since their obedience is shown to God, as our Lord Jesus Christ says: "He who hears you hears Me" (Luke 10:16). Therefore if anyone hearing the word does not rise at once, he is to be judged disobedient. But he who answers back incurs the charge of insubordination, and thus is not only guilty of disobedience, but also, by opening the way of answering back for others, is to be regarded as the destroyer of many. Yet if any murmurs, he too, as though not obeying heartily, must be considered disobedient. Therefore let his work be rejected, until his goodwill be made known. But up to what measure is obedience laid down? Up to death it is assuredly enjoined, since Christ obeyed the Father up to death for us. And this He suggests to us saying through the Apostle: "Let this mind be in you, which was also in Christ Jesus, Who though He was in the form of God, thought it no prize to snatch at to be equal with God; but emptied Himself, taking the form of a servant, and being found in fashion as a man, humbled Himself, being made obedient to the Father up to death, even the death of the cross" (Phil. 2:5–8). Thus nothing must be refused in their obedience by Christ's true disciples, however hard and difficult it be, but it must be seized with zeal, with gladness, since if obedience is not of this nature, it will not be pleasing to the Lord Who says: "And he who does not take his cross and follow Me, is not worthy of Me" (Matt. 10:38). And thus He says of the worthy disciple, "Where I am, there is My servant also with Me" (John 12:26).

II. Of Silence

The rule of silence is decreed to be carefully observed, since it is written: "But the nurture of righteousness is silence and peace" (Isa. 32:17). And thus, lest one be apprehended as guilty of much talking, it is needful that he keep silence, except for things profitable and necessary, since according to Scripture, in many words sin will not be lacking (Prov. 10:19). Therefore the Savior says: "By thy words thou shalt be justified, and by thy words thou shalt be condemned" (Matt. 12:37). Justly will they be damned who would not say just things when they could, but preferred to say with garrulous loquacity what is evil, unjust, irreverent, empty, harmful, dubious, false, provocative, disparaging, base, fanciful, blasphemous, rude, and tortuous. Therefore we must keep silence on these and kindred matters, and speak with care and prudence, lest either disparagements or swollen oppositions should break out in vicious garrulity.

III. Of Food and Drink

Let the monk's food be poor and taken in the evening, such as to avoid repletion, and their drink such as to avoid intoxication, so that it may both maintain life and not harm; vegetables, beans, flour mixed with water, together with the small bread of a loaf, lest the stomach be burdened and the mind confused. For indeed those who desire eternal rewards must only consider usefulness and use. Use of life must be moderated just as toil must be moderated, since this is true discretion, that the possibility of spiritual progress may be kept with a temperance that punishes the flesh. For if temperance exceeds measure, it will be a vice and not a virtue; for virtue maintains and retains many goods. Therefore we must fast daily, just as we must feed daily; and while we must eat daily, we must gratify the body more poorly and sparingly; since we must eat daily for the reason that we must go forward daily, pray daily, toil daily, and read daily.

IV. Of Poverty and of Overcoming Greed

By monks, to whom for Christ's sake the world is crucified and they to the world, greed must be avoided, when indeed it is reprehensible for them not only to have superfluities, but even to want them. In their case not property but will is required; and they, leaving all things and daily following the Lord Christ with the cross of fear, have treasures in heaven. Therefore, while they will have much in heaven, on earth they should be satisfied with the small possessions of utter need, knowing that greed is a leprosy for monks who copy the sons of the prophets, and for the disciple of Christ it is revolt and ruin, for the uncertain followers of the apostles also it is death. Thus then nakedness and disdain of riches are the first perfection of monks, but the second is the purging of vices, the third the most perfect and perpetual love of God and unceasing affection for things divine, which follows on the forgetfulness of earthly things. Since this is so, we have need of few things, according to the word of the Lord, or even of one. For few things are true necessities without which life cannot be led, or even one thing, like food according to the letter. But we require purity of feeling by the grace of God, that we may understand spiritually what are those few gifts of love which are offered to Martha by the Lord.

V. Of Overcoming Vanity

How dangerous vanity also may be is shown by a few words of the Savior, Who said to His disciples when they exulted in this vanity, "I saw Satan like lightning fall from heaven" (Luke 10:18), and Who says to the Jews when once they excused themselves, "But what is lofty among men is an abomination in the Lord's sight" (Luke 16:15). By these and by that most notorious case of the Pharisee who excused himself, we gather that vanity and proud self-esteem are the destroyer of all good things, when the Pharisee's vainly extolled goods perished and the publican's self-confessed sins vanished away. Then let no large word proceed from a monk's mouth, lest his own large labor perish.

VI. Of Chastity

A monk's chastity is indeed judged in his thoughts, and to him, along with the disciples who approached to hear, it is doubtless said by the Lord: "He who looks on a woman to lust after her has already defiled her in his heart" (Matt. 5:28). For while his vow is weighed by Him to Whom he is devoted, there is cause to fear lest He should find in the soul something to loathe, lest perhaps according to the opinion of St. Peter they have eyes full of wantonness and of adultery (cf. 2 Pet. 2:14). And what profit is it if he be virgin in body, if he be not virgin in mind? For God, being Spirit, dwells in the spirit and the mind which He has seen undefiled, in which there is no adulterous thought, no stain of a spirit polluted, and no spot of sin. . . .

VIII. Of Discretion

How necessary discretion is for monks is shown by the mistake of many, and indicated by the downfall of some, who beginning without discretion and passing their time without a sobering knowledge, have been unable to complete a praiseworthy life; since, just as error overtakes those who proceed without a path, so for those who live without discretion intemperance is at hand, and this is always the opposite of virtues which are placed in the mean between each extreme. Its onset is a matter of danger, when beside the straight way of discretion our foes place the stumbling-blocks of wickedness and the offences of various mistakes. Therefore we must pray God continually that He would bestow the light of true discretion to illumine this way, surrounded on every side by the world's thickest darkness, so that His true worshipers may be able to cross this darkness without error to Himself.

. . . Thus between the little and the excessive there is a reasonable measure in the midst, which ever recalls us from every superfluity on either side, and in every case posited provides what is universally fixed by human need, and spurns the unreasonable demand of superfluous desire. And this measure of true discretion, weighing all our actions in the scales of justice, in no wise allows us to err from what is just, or to suffer a mistake, if we ever follow straight behind it as our leader. For while we must always restrain ourselves from either side, according to that saying, "Keep yourselves from the right and from the left" (cf. Deut. 5:32), we must ever proceed straight forward by discretion, that is, by the light of God, while very often we say and sing the victorious psalmist's verse, "My God, enlighten my darkness, since in Thee I am rescued from temptation. For temptation is the life of man on earth" (Ps. 18:29; Job 7:1).

IX. Of Mortification

The chief part of the monks' Rule is mortification, since indeed they are enjoined in Scripture, "Do nothing without counsel" (Sir. 32:24). Thus if nothing is to be done without counsel, everything must be asked for by counsel. Thus we are enjoined through Moses also, "Ask thy father and he will show thee, thy elders and they will tell thee" (Deut. 32:7). But though this training seem hard to the hard-hearted, namely that a man should always hang upon the lips of another, yet by those who are fixed in their fear of God it will be found pleasant and safe, if it is kept wholly and not in part, since nothing is more pleasant than safety of conscience and nothing safer than exoneration of the soul, which none can provide for himself by his own efforts, since it properly belongs to the judgment of others. For what the judge's examination has already tried preserves from the fear of censure, and on him is laid the weight of another's burden, and he bears all the peril that he undertakes; for, as it is written, the peril of the judge is greater than that of the accused. So anyone who has always asked, if he follows will never err, since if the other's reply has erred, there will be no error in the faith of him who believes and the toil of him who obeys, nor will they lack the reward of his asking. For if he has considered anything by himself when he ought to have asked, he is proved guilty of error in this very fact that he dared to judge when he ought to have been judged; even though it turn out right, it will be reckoned to him as wrong, since he has departed from the right course in this; for the man to whose duty it belongs only to obey presumes to judge nothing by himself.

Then, since this is so, monks must everywhere beware of a proud independence, and learn true lowliness as they obey without murmuring and hesitation, that according to the Lord's word they may feel the yoke of Christ pleasant and His burden light. Otherwise, while they are learning the lowliness of Christ, they will not feel the pleasure of His yoke and the lightness of His burden. For lowliness of heart is the repose of the soul when wearied with vices and toils, and its only refuge from so many evils, and insofar as it is wholly drawn to the meditation of this from so many errant and empty things without, so far does it enjoy repose and refreshment within, with the result that even bitter things are sweet to it, and things before considered hard and toilsome it feels to be plain and easy, and mortification also, which is unbearable to the proud and hard-hearted, becomes his comfort who takes pleasure only in what is lowly and mild. But we must know that neither this bliss of martyrdom nor any other benefit that follows can be perfectly fulfilled by any, save him who has given particular attention to this, that he be not found unready. For if, in following this pursuit, he has wished to observe or nourish any of his own desires, at once occupied and wholly confused by concern for these intrusions, he will not always be able to follow thankfully where the commandment leads, nor can the disorderly and unthankful perform as is his duty.

Thus there is a threefold scheme of mortification: not to disagree in mind, not to speak as one pleases with the tongue, not to go anywhere with complete freedom. Its part is ever to say to a senior, however adverse his instructions, "Not as I will but as thou wilt" (Matt. 26:39), following the example of the Lord and Savior, Who says, "I came down from heaven, not to do My will, but the will of Him Who sent Me, the Father" (John 6:38).

Communal Rule

[A diversity of faults should be cured by the application of a diversity of penance. Therefore, my dearest brethren]

I. It has been ordained, my dearest brethren, by the holy fathers that we make confession before meat or before entering our beds or whenever it is opportune [of all failings, not only mortal ones, but also of minor omissions] since confession and penance free from death. Therefore not even the very small sins are to be omitted from confession, since, as it is written, He who omits small things gradually declines [so that confession should be made before meat, before entering our beds, or whenever it is opportune to make it].

Thus him who has not kept grace at table and has not responded Amen, it is ordained to correct with six blows. [These were inflicted with a leather strap on the hand]. Likewise him who has spoken while eating, not because of the wants of another brother, it is ordained to correct with six. [If one has called anything his own, with six blows.] And him who has not blessed the spoon with which he sups [with six blows], and him who has spoken with a shout, that is has talked in a louder tone than the usual, with six blows.

II. If he has not blessed the lamp, that is when it is lighted by a younger brother and is not presented to a senior for his blessing, with six blows. If he has called anything his own, with six blows. [If he has done some idle work, with six blows.] Let him who has cut the table with a knife be corrected with ten blows.

Whoever of the brethren, to whom the care of cooking or serving has been entrusted, has spilt any drop, it is ordained to correct him by prayer in church after the end of the office, so that the brethren pray for him. Let him who has forgotten the prostration at the synaxis, that is at the office, namely the prostration in church after the end of each psalm, do penance likewise. In the same manner let him who has lost the crumbs be corrected by prayer in church; yet this small penance is only to be assigned to him, if it is something small that he has spilt.

IV. Him who through a cough has not chanted well at the beginning of a psalm, it is ordained to correct with six blows. Likewise him who has bitten the cup of salvation with his teeth, with six blows. Him who has not followed the order for the sacrifice [for celebrating], with six blows. [A priest when celebrating who has not trimmed his nails, and a deacon, whose beard has not been shaved, him who has receives the sacrifice, approaches the chalice, straight from farm-work, with six blows.] And him who is smiling at the synaxis, that is, at the office of prayers, with six blows; if his laughter has broken out aloud, with an imposition, unless it has happened pardonably. [A priest, when celebrating, and a deacon, who are holding the sacrifice, should beware lest they wander with roving eyes; and if they neglect this, they must be corrected with six blows. He who has forgotten his chrismal when hurrying out to some work, with five times five blows; if he has dropped it on the ground in a field, and found it at once, with five times ten blows; if he has hung it on a tree, with thrice ten, if it remains there overnight, with an imposition]. He who with unclean hands receives the blessed bread, with twelve blows. He who forgets to make the oblation right until they go to Mass, with a hundred blows.

THE RULE OF A CERTAIN FATHER TO THE VIRGINS

From *The Rule of a Certain Father to the Virgins*, attributed to Waldebert, translated by Jo Ann McNamara and John Halborg. Toronto, Ontario: Peregrina Publishing Co., 1993, 2nd edition.

Abbot Waldebert of Luxeuil (ca. 629–670) combines elements from the Rule of Benedict and the Columbanus Rule in his *Rule for Virgins*. The following Merovingian Rule was written for monastic women living in double monasteries around the middle of the seventh century, where men and women occupied separate living quarters, but shared common functions in schools and divine service. It shows, among other things, that the women were required to perform manual labor with careful prescription for routine extra-cloistral activities. Waldebert actively recruited Frankish noblewomen to the monastic life in the seventh century and his Rule illustrates the practices under his pastoral guidance. The selection highlights the qualities and skills needed by the abbess, the charity required of all, as well as the importance of labor and poverty, each central to the monastic life.

How the abbess ought to behave to the monastery.
The abbess of a monastery ought not so much to be noble by birth as noble by wisdom and holiness. Her words to the souls she is instructing should glow with just erudition and never be contradicted by her own actions. In fact, the subjects of prelates tend to imitate their acts more readily than they give heed to their teaching. Thus she should twine holy words with holy deeds so that those who imitate her vocal teaching will also imitate her active behavior. Thus her work should in no way contradict her voice, for words alone are not enough to bear fruit. Therefore she should be so adorned with voice and works that the work confirms the voice and the voice the work. She should be continent, counting chastity as her flower, so that, praised by every tongue, her example is imitable by all. She should be benevolent to all with charity so that the hearts of all the faithful rejoice. She should lead the

way in solicitude for pilgrims and guests and thoughtful care for the
sick and in the needy poor with her wealth. Thus she should correct
the sloth of delinquents so that they turn their lascivious and confused
minds to religious worship. She should distribute gifts of kindness merci-
fully though she must not provide comfort to wrong-doing from excessive kindness. She should be good to those who deserve goodness
and bad to the bad, even to whipping, mediating all she does with knowledge, as the Psalmist says in prayer, "Teach me good judgement and
knowledge, O Lord" (Ps. 119:60). Thus the abbess must take care on
both sides lest, on the one hand, she nourish vice in the hearts of her
subjects by excessive kindness, or, by excessive austerity of discipline,
she cause those whom soft words might heal to be torn away by rigid
correction. Therefore, let her provide mild persuasion to the careless as
she would administer a healing cure as an antidote for their health. For
indeed she must provide health to the sick by encouragement so that
they who began to act (well) shall turn to the better even to the end.
For there is no point in beginning if those who begin good work do
not strive to persevere. Therefore the mother has as many souls as she
has daughters under her control. She must learn the habits of each of
them so that she will know how to repress the vice in each. She will have
such providence for all that piety shall not give way to discipline nor
discipline to piety. Let her act with every care so that she will receive
the profit she has earned for every gain and, whenever she is removed
from the corruption of the present life, she will receive the price of her
labour, for her compensation will be increased by as much as she contributed to the conquest of the enemy. . . .

5. On loving one another and obeying one another.

Nuns in a monastery must take as much care to love one another in
Christ as the Lord shows through the Gospel of John, who said, "This
is my command, that ye love one another. For greater love hath no man
than that a man lay down his life for his friends" (John 15:13–14); and
again, "By this shall all men know that ye are my disciples if ye have
love to one another" (John 13:35). Therefore we order you to love one
another, so that we may save one another. Thus through mutual love
we imitate Him "Who loved us" as the Apocalypse says, "and washed

us from our sins with His own blood" (Rev. 1:5). Therefore if a sister loves a sister because of Christ she will not drive Christ from her for the sake of temporal love. For love of neighbor, which is true and according to Christ, cannot work evil. The neighbor is therefore to be loved with no carnal affection but with the service of piety. She is loved in purity, she is loved in religion, she is loved in clemency, she is loved in charity: in all, that is always found through love of Christ but love remains not according to the world but according to God. For thus the Lord commands, "Thou shalt love thy neighbor as thyself" (Matt. 22:39). If a sister loves a sister as herself, she will never incur the stain of sin but will take the eternal prize adorned with piety and love. Therefore keep love always in the heart that extinguishes the envious poison of the ancient enemy which through deception opened the gate to death to the primordial protoplasm, as is written, "Through envy the devil came into the world" (Wisd. of Sol. 2:24). The neighbor is loved lest by the bloody stain of hate she incur the crime of homicide as John the Apostle witnesses saying, "Whoever hates his brother is a murderer" (1 John 3:15). The neighbor is loved lest through encouraging discord to be retained, she is not released from the chains of her own crimes. As the Lord witnesses in the Gospel saying, "If ye forgive not men their trespasses, neither will your father forgive you your trespasses" (Matt. 6:15). So in forgiving our debtors we are released from debt by the Almighty. "Give and it shall be given unto you" (Luke 6:30). Oh what a just exchange! Oh what pious mercy! Giving you receive; taking you give. No increment of brawling or nutriment is kept but as the Apostle exhorts saying "Be ye kind one to another, tender-hearted, forgiving one another, even as God, for Christ's sake, hath forgiven you" (Eph. 4:32). We should ask nothing to be given to us but what we are asked to give. Thus we say praying, "Forgive us our debts as we forgive our debtors" (Matt. 6:12). By forgiving our debtors we are freed from debt. Therefore let us set free our neighbors through love and fondness so that God will free us from our crimes with piety and mercy. Amen. . . .

12. In what way should the daily manual labor be carried out?

Except on feast days, work will always be done either to supply needs or to have something to give to the poor. Manual labor must be arranged so that the fruit of reading is not omitted. Thus work must be ordered at the proper time and then left for divine reading. Manual labor takes priority from the second hour and comes to an end in the ninth hour. Reading is customary from the ninth hour (but) if anyone has work of her own to be done—mending or washing clothes or anything of that sort—she may do it with the permission of the abbess or prioress. If there is more pressing work at hand, like picking ripe fruit, or the summer heat is overwhelming, the abbess may make adjustments at will. Thus, if time allows or the weight of the labor wearies, they may rest at the sixth hour as she thinks fit and, after the rest, the work will begin again until refection or even to Vespers. It will be shared among all as the abbess, if she is present, determines or the prioress to whom she has given up the task. She shall permit absolutely no *monacha* to leave for some idle excuse but only after investigating the need. Let her be bound by the memory that the work of God lies in manual labor: that is, while externally occupied by manual labor, her interior mind sweetens the time by meditating on the psalms with her tongue or considering remembered scripture. And she who violates this rule with idle gossip will be punished with the penalty of silence. If there should be penitents, they must make the fires in the schola in pairs for a week. Similarly, each Saturday, penitents should wash the heads of every sister or prepare the baths to be used on solemn festivals or do any other particularly difficult job. Thus they shall make their minds humble and their hearts contrite through fear of the Lord so that God's mercy shall more speedily cleanse them of their crimes. And when she is going to this work she will chant the chapter, "Let the beauty of the Lord God be upon us and establish thou the work of our hands upon us; yea, the work of our hands, establish thou it" (Ps. 90:17). And indeed when the work is done she will begin the chapter, "God bless us, our Lord, and all the ends of the earth shall fear Him" (Ps. 67:8). The women who grind and bake the flour will do the work together taking turns so that there are never less than three when there is need to speak. And if they must remain (in the bakery), there should be no less than four and the senior of them should be prioress, whose religion is trustworthy so that she can have license for speaking. And the senior among them shall show the bread they made in turn to the cellaress who will take all care is taken that nothing reprehensible happens among them. Likewise, those who live in the brewery to make the beer will have a senior among them as prioress who will take every precaution as we said for the bakers. And indeed we appoint three or more cooks for the weekly cooking as may be needed in a single week; lest indiscriminate labor is imposed until she who should have earned a reward gets penalized for grumbling instead. On entering, they should ask all the other sisters to pray for them and, praying, they should say, "Our help is in the Lord's name who made heaven and earth" (Ps. 124:8) and "Help us, O God of our Salvation" (Ps. 79:9). Going out they wash the feet of all the sisters and they should return all the vessels which they needed to use, washed, to the prioress. Similarly they should ask prayers for themselves and say in this verse praying, "Thou Lord hast helped me and comforted me" (Ps. 86:17). Any single negligence by the cook or cellaress must be corrected by twenty-five slaps daily lest a few minor faults left unattended should develop into incorrigible habits. . . .

17. How no *monacha* ought to claim anything in the monastery as her own.

She must have nothing of her own in the monastery but rather have given up all in the Lord's name. What faithful soul to whom the world is crucified and she to the world would claim anything of her own from the things of this world? Indeed being dead to the world, why should she somehow begin to live in the world through any desire for temporal things or greed for wealth, who through contempt of the world has begun to live for God? Therefore all *monachas* must amputate this vice at the root so that nothing, either clothing or shoes or anything, may be called her own or be said to be hers, except insofar as by order of the abbess she may be told to take charge of something and guard it for another which she may not have as property or under her own control. And she may not presume to give what has been commended to her by the abbess, that is, for present necessities like clothing to anyone else, or exchange it later except as the abbess may order. What worldly thing might she confer on another sister who has placed herself entirely in the abbess's power according to Christ? For all things that they have in the monastery are held in common as we read in the acts of the Apostles, "And they had all things in common" (Acts 4:32). Thus having all in common, they can give or accept nothing except by order of the abbess lest by greed and rashness they fall into the evil snare and be numbered among the companions of Judas the traitor, the only apostle who is said to have had a purse when there was a need for buying and selling. And if this vice ensnare any of the sisters into crime and, after a first, second or third correction, she does not amend, she must submit to the discipline of the Rule.

THE CAROLINGIAN REFORM

BENEDICT OF ANIANE, BY ARDO

From *The Emperor's Monk: Contemporary Life of Benedict of Aniane, by Ardo*, translated with an introduction by Allen Cabaniss. Ilfracombe, Devon: A. H. Stockwell, 1979.

The following selection is from Ardo, also known as Smaragdus (ca. 783–843), the biographer of Benedict of Aniane (750–821), who was a reformer, abbot, and chief counselor to Emperor Charlemagne. Benedict of Aniane created a concordance of all available Rules on religious life in the ninth century and recommended the *Rule of St. Benedict* as the exemplar for Imperial reform carried out under Louis the Pious. Benedict's support of the Rule of Benedict made it the accepted monastic Rule in the West and therefore exerted profound influence on the history of Rules. Almost nothing is known of Ardo's life except that he was a monk at Aniane during Benedict's abbacy. The *Life of Benedict of Aniane* was written between 824–26 for the monks of Inde who requested a history of Benedict after his death. Here, Ardo presents himself as a witness to the contemporary monastic culture and those things Benedict of Aniane sought to correct and the virtues he intended to inculcate.

[Chapter] 35:4. There were many who consulted the abbot about direction of the realm, about disposition of provinces, and about their own advantage. No one in fact had such compassion on the miseries of the afflicted; no one revealed to the emperor the needs of monks as he did.

Benedict was an advocate of the wretched, but a father of monks; a comforter of the poor, but a teacher of monks. He provided the food of life for rich people, but he inculcated the discipline of the Rule upon the minds of monks.

Chapter 36:1. The emperor therefore set Benedict over all monasteries in his realm, that as he had instructed Aquitaine and Gothia in the standard of salvation, so also might he imbue Frankland with a salutary example. Many monasteries had once been established in the Rule, but little by little firmness had grown lax and regularity of the Rule had almost perished. That there might be one wholesome usage for all monasteries, as there was one profession by all, the emperor ordered the fathers of monasteries to assemble with as many monks as possible. They were in session for many days. When all had come together, Benedict elucidated obscure points to all as he discussed the entire Rule; he made clear doubtful points; he swept away old errors; he confirmed useful practices and arrangements. He presented decisions of the Rule and questionable points with keen result, as well as practices the Rule did not mention. Everyone gave assent. Benedict then prepared for the emperor a chapter by chapter decree for confirmation to enjoin observance in all monasteries of his realm. We refer the inquiring reader to that document.

36:2. Louis appointed inspectors for each monastery to oversee whether those practices that were enjoined were observed and to transmit the wholesome standard to those unaware of it. By the aid of divine mercy the work was happily accomplished. All monasteries were returned to a degree of unity as if taught by one teacher in one place. Uniform measure in drink and food, in vigils and singing, was decreed to be observed by all. Since Benedict established observance of the Rule throughout other monasteries, he instructed his own at Inde so that monks coming from other regions might not engage in the noisy conversation to which they were accustomed, but might see the standard and discipline of the Rule portrayed in usage, walk, and dress of the monks at Inde.

Chapter 37:1. Because of the indiscreet warmth of many, the unwarranted tepidness of some, and the obtuse sensibility of those with less capacity, Benedict determined a boundary and gave to all an arrangement to be observed, restraining some from seeking superfluous exertions, commanding others to shake off sluggishness, admonishing still others to fulfill at least what they did know. He ordered many things in conformity with the Rule. But there are a great many matters demanded in daily practice about which the Rule is silent. Yet by them a monk's habit is adorned as if with jewels and without which it appears to be careless, monotonous, and disorganized. . . .

38:5. The practice of many had in the past caused them also to dress differently. The cowls of some hung down to their ankles. God's man therefore instituted a uniform style to be worn by all monks: the length should not extend more than two cubits or reach to the knees. Out of necessity he conceded beyond what the Rule decrees: two woolen shirts, pants, leather cloaks and coverings, and two copes. Whatever he observed as necessary to diminish evasion by any pretext, he conceded and allowed.

38:6. In a letter to the emperor, Benedict gave his opinion on those matters which the Rule directs but which for good reason remained untried, as well as on those matters on which it was silent but which were usefully introduced. He directed his desire toward observance of the Rule; it was his greatest study that nothing might escape his knowledge. Consequently he interrogated minutely those whom he found to be expert, whether living nearby or at a distance. Those who came into these parts on their way to Monte Cassino he asked to collect not only what they heard, but also what they saw. Because of his love of knowledge, anyone who might unfold something new to him he received without delay, with humility, and chatted with him without awe.

38:7. Even so he could not learn all the hidden meanings of the Rule. With everyone (not with novices, of course, but with wise persons) he would make it clear that he learned new and unheard of matters not only from learned people, but also from simpler ones. He caused a book to be compiled from the Rules of various fathers, so that blessed Benedict's Rule might be foremost in the minds of all. He gave orders to read it all the time in the morning at assembly. To demonstrate to contentious persons that nothing worthless or useless was set forth by blessed Benedict, but that his Rule was sustained by the Rules of others, he compiled another book of statements culled from other Rules. To it he gave the title, *Harmony of the Rules*. Statements in agreement with blessed Benedict's book were added to show that the latter was obviously foremost. To it he joined another book from the sermons of holy teachers. These were presented for exhortation of monks. It he ordered read all the time at the evening assemblies.

Chapter 39:1. Perceiving that some men panted with all their might to acquire monasteries of monks and strove not only with petitions, but also with money, to obtain them; perceiving, too, that monastic expenses were being sequestered by them for selfish purposes; and perceiving that in that way some monasteries were being destroyed and others secured by secular clergy after the monks were driven away, Benedict went to the most pious emperor and pressed him with supplications to ban clergy from contentions of this kind and set the exiled monks free from this danger. The most glorious emperor gave consent and decreed that all monasteries in his realm where there were regular abbots be enumerated, By charter he ordered that they remain unchanged for all time; he sealed that charter with his ring. Thus he stripped the greed of many and at the same time relieved the anxiety of the monks.

39:2. Certain monasteries were employed for secular burdens and for military service. They had reached such dire poverty that both food and clothing were lacking to the monks. Considering that, the most pious king, at the aforesaid man's suggestion, gave order to relieve them as much as possible so that nothing might be lacking to God's servants. For this alleviation they gladly prayed to God for the emperor, his children, and the pious establishment of the entire realm. Those monasteries that remained under canonical authority he arranged separately so they could live according to the Rule, but the rest he granted to the abbot.

THE CLUNIAC REFORM

THE FOUNDATION CHARTER OF THE ORDER OF CLUNY, SEPTEMBER 11, 909 A.D.

From *Select Historical Documents of the Middle Ages*, edited and translated by Ernest F. Henderson, pp. 329–33. London: Bell and Sons, 1892.

William of Aquitaine (ca. 863–918) founded a reformed monastery at the abbey of Cluny in 909. He used his prestige to establish a "free" monastery which protected Cluny from any secular and ecclesiastic interference which contributed to a decline in monastic discipline in many communities. The foundation charter, presented here, promotes a more strict adherence to the *Rule of Benedict* and the free elections established in the Rule. Cluny grew to become the most powerful and influential monastic order in the Middle Ages. The foundation and flowering of Cluny most certainly lay the foundations for future monastic renewal in both its free canonical elections and the model of loose federation of monastic houses following the same customs and liturgical practices.

To all right thinkers it is clear that the providence of God has so provided for certain rich men that, by means of their transitory possessions, if they use them well, they may be able to merit everlasting rewards. As to which thing, indeed, the divine word, showing it to be

105

possible and altogether advising it, says: "The riches of a man are the redemption of his soul" (Prov. 13:8). I, William, count and duke by the grace of God, diligently pondering this, and desiring to provide for my own safety while I am still able, have considered it advisable nay, most necessary, that from the temporal goods which have been conferred upon me I should give some little portion for the gain of my soul. I do this, indeed, in order that I who have thus increased in wealth may not, perchance, at the last be accused of having spent all in caring for my body, but rather may rejoice, when fate at last shall snatch all things away, in having reserved something for myself. Which end, indeed, seems attainable by no more suitable means than that, following the precept of Christ: "I will malice his poor my friends" (Luke 16:9), and making the act not a temporary but a lasting one, I should support at my own expense a congregation of monks. And this is my trust, this my hope, indeed, that although I myself am unable to despise all things, nevertheless, by receiving those who despise the world, whom I believe to be righteous, I may receive the reward of the righteous. Therefore be it known to all who live in the unity of the faith and who await the mercy of Christ, and to those who shall succeed them and who shall continue to exist until the end of the world, that, for the love of God and of our Savior Jesus Christ, I hand over from my own rule to the holy apostles, Peter, namely, and Paul, the possessions over which I hold sway, the town of Cluny, namely, with the court and demesne manor, and the church in honor of St. Mary the mother of God and of St. Peter the prince of the apostles, together with all the things pertaining to it, the vills, indeed, the chapels, the serfs of both sexes, the vines, the fields, the meadows, the woods, the waters and their outlets, the mills, the incomes and revenues, what is cultivated and what is not, all in their entirety. Which things are situated in or about the country of Macon, each one surrounded by its own bounds. I give, moreover, all these things to the aforesaid apostles—I, William, and my wife Ingelberga— first for the love of God; then for the soul of my lord king Odo, of my father and my mother; for myself and my wife—for the salvation, namely, of our souls and bodies; and not least for that of Ava who left me these things in her will; for the souls also of our brothers and sisters and nephews, and of all our relatives of both sexes; for our faithful ones who adhere to our service; for the advancement, also, and integrity of the catholic religion. Finally, since all of us Christians are held together by one bond of love and faith, let this donation be for all, for the orthodox, namely, of past, present or future times. I give these things, moreover, with this understanding, that in Cluny a regular monastery shall be constructed in honour of the holy apostles Peter and Paul, and that there the monks shall congregate and live according to the Rule of St. Benedict, and that they shall possess, hold, have and order these same things unto all time. In such wise, however, that the venerable house of prayer which is there shall be faithfully frequented with vows and supplications, and that celestial converse shall be sought and striven after with all desire and with the deepest ardor; and also that there shall be sedulously directed to God prayers, beseeching and exhortations as well for me as for all, according to the order in which mention has been made of them above. And let the monks themselves, together with all the aforesaid possessions, be under the power and dominion of the abbot Berno, who, as long as he shall live, shall preside over them regularly according to his knowledge and ability. But after his death, those same monks shall have power and permission to elect any one of their order whom they please as abbot and rector, following the will of God and the Rule promulgated by St. Benedict, in such wise that neither by the intervention of our own or of any other power may they be impeded from making a purely canonical election. Every five years, moreover, the aforesaid monks shall pay to the church of the apostles at Rome ten shillings to supply them with lights; and they shall have the protection of those same apostles and the defense of the Roman pontiff; and those monks may, with their whole heart and soul, according to their ability and knowledge, build up the aforesaid place. We will, further, that in our times and in those of our successors, according as the opportunities and possibilities of that place shall allow, there shall daily, with the greatest zeal be performed there works of mercy towards the poor, the needy, strangers and pilgrims. It has pleased us also to insert in this document that, from this day, those same monks there congregated shall be subject neither to our yoke, nor to that of our relatives, nor to the sway of the royal might, nor to that of any earthly power. And, through God and all his saints, and by the

awful day of judgment, I warn and abjure that no one of the secular
princes, no count, no bishop whatever, not the pontiff of the aforesaid
Roman see, shall invade the property of these servants of God, or
alienate it, or diminish it, or exchange it, or give it as a benefice to any
one, or constitute any prelate over them against their will. And that
such unhallowed act may be more strictly prohibited to all rash and
wicked men, I subjoin the following, giving force to the warning. I adjure
ye, oh holy apostles and glorious princes of the world, Peter and Paul,
and thee, oh supreme pontiff of the apostolic see that, through the canonical and apostolic authority which ye have received from God, ye do
remove from participation in the holy church and in eternal life, the
robbers and invaders and alternators of these possessions which I do give
to ye with joyful heart and ready will; and be ye protectors and defen-
ders of the aforementioned place of Cluny and of the servants of God
abiding there, and of all these possessions on account of the clemency
and mercy of the most holy Redeemer. If any one, which Heaven forbid, and which, through the mercy of God and the protection of the
apostles I do not think will happen, whether he be a neighbor or a stranger, no matter what his condition or power, should, through any kind
of wile, attempt to do any act of violence contrary to this deed of gift
which we have ordered to be drawn up for love of almighty God and
for reverence of the chief apostles Peter and Paul: first, indeed, let him
incur the wrath of almighty God, and let God remove him from the land
of the living and wipe out his name from the book of life, and let his
portion be with those who said to the Lord God: Depart from us; and,
with Dathan and Abiron whom the earth, opening its jaws, swallowed
up, and hell absorbed while still alive, let him incur everlasting damnation. And being made a companion of Judas let him be kept thrust
down there with eternal tortures, and, lest it seem to human eyes that
he pass through the present world with impunity, let him experience in
his own body, indeed, the torments of future damnation, sharing the
double disaster with Heliodorus and Antiochus, of whom one being
coerced with sharp blows scarcely escaped alive; and the other, struck
down by the divine will, his members putrefying and swarming with
vermin, perished most miserably. And let him be a partaker with other
sacrilegious persons who presume to plunder the treasure of the house

of God; and let him, unless he come to his senses, have as enemy and as the one who will refuse him entrance into the blessed paradise, the key-bearer of the whole hierarchy of the church, and, joined with the latter, St. Paul; both of whom, if he had wished, he might have had as most holy mediators for him. But as far as the worldly law is concerned, he shall be required, the judicial power compelling him, to pay a hundred pounds of gold to those whom he has harmed; and his attempted attack, being frustrated, shall have no effect at all. But the validity of this deed of gift, endowed with all authority, shall always remain inviolate and unshaken, together with the stipulation subjoined. Done publicly in the city of Bourges. I, William, commanded this act to be made and drawn up, and confirmed it with my own hand.

(Signed by Ingelberga and a number of bishops and nobles.)

THE TWELFTH-CENTURY MONASTIC RENEWAL

The twelfth century saw a renewed interest in the monastic life. Those folks seeking a religious life re-interpreted the *Rule of Benedict* and revitalized the *Rule of St. Augustine* in a new light within a new social context. In many ways, the renewed enthusiasm for the regular life was motivated by the Gregorian reform, which emphasized a return to the Early church for its reforming ideals. In the monastic world, a return to the foundations led to a re-examination of the Desert Elders and their emphasis on solitude and manual labor and a rejection of the world. Thus, many of the Orders, while taking the *Rule of Benedict* or the *Rule of Augustine*, interpreted these *Regula* in a new light which places more emphasis on retreat from the world to a desert, a desire for participation in the eremitical life, even in community, and a renewal of the spiritual communion through *lectio divina*.

THE CARTHUSIANS

Translations from Robin Bruce Lockhart, *Listening to Silence: An Anthology of Carthusian Writings*, pp. 3–10, xv–xvii. London: Darton, Longman, Todd, 1997.

The Carthusians, founded by Bruno of Cologne (ca. 1030–1101), who, in 1084, retreated to a piece of land situated near the Alps of Dauphiné named Chartreuse, not far from Grenoble, France, a rocky snow-covered terrain. The Carthusians lived a quasi-communal life, each with their own cell in which to work and pray, with much of their time spent alone. The following selections include a letter from Bruno written in 1099 and official Statutes of the order, begun after 1128 by Abbot Guigo. St. Bruno's letter is to friend Raoul after leaving the cathedral school of Reims; it is a rare letter from two surviving examples. Carefully reading Bruno's letter allows for a deeper understanding of the spiritual foundations for contemplative life as well as his understanding of God, humanity, and how best to develop a relationship with the divine. The statutes give emphasis and a deeper understanding to the Carthusian approach to the solitary life lived communally.

St. Bruno's Letter

Letter to Raoul le Verd, Provost of the Rheims Chapter (written circa 1099 A.D.)
To the Venerable Raoul, Provost of Rheims, in a spirit of most pure charity Bruno addresses his salutations.

1. In you there shines the fidelity of our old and solid friendship, all the more remarkable and praiseworthy that it is so rare to come across among men. Despite the distances and years which have separated us, never for a moment have I felt my affection for you, old friend, wane. The great warmth of your letters reveals to me once again the tenderness of your friendship. Your many kindnesses bestowed with such prodigality upon my person and upon Brother Bernard on my behalf and also many further signs all provide further proof. My gratitude cannot reach the heights you deserve, but it gushes from a crystalline source of affection and in reply to your overwhelming kindness.

2. A traveler who on previous occasions has proved reliable left quite a long time ago as bearer of a letter from me to you: as he has never yet reappeared it seemed to me sensible to send a member of our community in order to keep you informed of what has been happening to me.

As it is difficult to tell all in writing, he will be able to tell you everything in detail verbally.

3. I would like you to be aware—for perhaps it is not a question of
indifference to you—that my bodily health is good (if only it were the
same for the soul!). As regards external matters, all goes as well as I
could wish. But in truth in my prayers I await that divine mercy which
would heal all my inner miseries and crown my inner desires.

4. I am living in Calabria with some religious brothers, a number of
whom are highly cultured and who constantly keep a holy watch for
the return of the Master so that they can open themselves up to him as
soon as he knocks. I dwell in a wilderness well away from any dwellings
of men. How can I tell you in full of its charm, its wholesome air, the
vast arid beautiful plain which stretches itself out between the mountain ranges, with its grassy meadows and its beflowered pastures? How
can I describe the views of the hills, which slope gently all around; the
shady secrets of the valleys where there is an abundance of streams, not
to mention well-watered gardens and orchards planted with various trees?

5. But why do I spend my time telling you of these things? For the wise
man there are other pleasures, infinitely sweeter and more valuable because of divine origin. However, when the rigor of regular discipline
and spiritual exercises imposes burdens on fragile souls, the latter find
relief and repose in these charms. For a bow that remains stretched too
long without relaxation, loses its strength and is no longer fit for use.

6. What advantages and delights solitude and the silence of the hermitage bring to those who love it, they alone know who have experience of
it. They can dwell apart and attend without interruption to the cultivation of the seeds of virtue and happily eat of the fruit of Paradise.
   There alone can one actively seek a clear vision of the Heavenly
Spouse, wounded by love, and behold God. There alone we are fully
occupied and we grow still in that peace that the world knows not and
with joy in the Holy Ghost. Remember fair Rachel in all her elegance,
she whom Jacob preferred even if she gave him fewer children than

Leah. Indeed the offspring of contemplation are less numerous than those of active life; nevertheless Joseph and Benjamin were preferred by their father to their other brothers. The better part was chosen by Mary of which she will not be deprived.

7. Think of the lovely Shunemite, the only maiden in Israel worthy to embrace to her bosom the aging David and to restore his waning affection. And you, my very dear brother, do you not love God above all else, so that grasped in his embrace, you are burning with a love quite divine? Then the glory of the world would fill you with disgust and you would reject the riches so overladen with cares and so burdensome; the pleasures themselves would grow repugnant, for they are no less harmful to the body than to the soul.

8. In your wisdom you will be aware of he who said, "In he who loves the world and what is in the world, that is to say the pleasures of the flesh, the covetousness of the eyes and ambition—the love of God the Father is not to be found." And similarly, "He who is the friend of this world thereby becomes the enemy of God." But then is there a worse sin or signs of a spirit out of order and in a state of collapse, an attitude more deadly or more lamentable than to rise up against him whose power is irresistible and whose justice is certain and to wish to declare war on him? Are we stronger than he is? Today his goodness ever invites us to show ourselves penitent but does that mean to say that he will not in the end punish the insult committed by scorning this offer? What could be more contrary, more opposed to reason, to justice, to nature, than to love the creature more than the Creator, to pursue passing advantages rather than eternity itself or things terrestrial rather than celestial?

9. What are we then to do, oh my well-beloved friend? What if not to believe the divine counsels, to believe in that Truth which can never deceive? It in effect gives this advice to the world: "Come to me, all you who are in labor, and are crushed beneath the burden and I will comfort you." Is it not a ghastly and useless torture to be tormented by one's desires, to be constantly bruising oneself against the cares and

anguish, the fear and suffering begotten by these desires? What burden is heavier than that which drags down the spirit from the summit of its sublime dignity towards the lowest depths of total wickedness? Oh my dear brother, flee away from all these troubles and anxieties and leave the tempest of this world to that harbour where there is peace and rest.

10. You well know what Wisdom has said: "He who does not renounce all that he has cannot be my disciple." Is it not noble, useful and pleasant to be in one's school under the teaching of the Holy Spirit, and there to learn that divine philosophy which alone bestows true happiness? Surely this is dear to all?

11. So it is therefore of the greatest importance that you examine your situation with all possible wisdom and prudence. If the love that God bestows on you seems insufficient, if the allurement of such reward does not attract you, do at least allow yourself to be convinced by the fear of inescapable punishment.

12. You know the vow which binds you, and to whom you are so bound. Omnipotent and awe-inspiring is he to whom you have made the vow to give yourself as an offering agreeable in his eyes: you have not the right to break the word you have pledged to him and it is not in your interest to do so for he cannot allow men to dishonor him with impunity.

13. You whom I love have a good memory. Remember the day we were both together with one-eyed Foulques in the little garden at Adam's house where I was then lodging. We talked of deceitful pleasures, the perishable riches of this world, and the joys of unending glory. At that moment, inflamed by divine love, we promised to make vows and we promptly decided to quit this transient life in order that we might pursue the eternal realities and to accept the habit of a monk. All this would have been done at once had not Foulques then left for Rome. We put off the execution of our plan until the time of his return. He was delayed, other forces came into play, his courage cooled off and his fervor waned.

14. What is there to be done, my very dear friend, except to discharge yourself as soon as you can of this debt? Otherwise, for so grave and so prolonged a breach of your word you will incur the wrath of the omnipotent God, and thereby terrible suffering. What great man of this world would allow any one of his subjects to cheat him of a gift he had promised to make him, especially if he attached exceptional value to it? So I do ask you to put your confidence not in my words but rather in those of the prophet and in those of the Holy Spirit. "Make vows to the Lord your God and fulfil them, all of you who bring gifts to him who cuts short the breath of princes and fills the kings of the earth with terror." Listen to your God; he cuts short the breath of princes. Listen to him who fills the kings of the earth with terror. Why is the Holy Spirit so insistent about this if it is not to persuade you to fulfil the vow which you promised? Why fulfil only with regret what will not involve you in any loss or diminution of what you have? It is you who will find therein the greater advantages and not he to whom you will be paying his dues.

15. Do not be detained by the deceitful charms of wealth so incapable of banishing unhappiness nor by the dazzle of your position as Provost which it is so difficult to perform without putting your soul in grave danger. You are established as the custodian of other men's property and not its proprietor; if you divert it to your own personal use—please do not allow my words to irritate you—it is as odious as it is unjust. If luxury and splendor allure you and you maintain a household of considerable magnificence, are you not going to be obliged to make up for the insufficiency of the income which you have earned by honest means to find methods of depriving some of what you are paying to others? To do so is neither moral nor to show oneself generous, for nothing is generous unless it is basically just.

16. I would like to see your love encompass one more thing. His Grace the Archbishop has great confidence in the advice you give and relies upon it. It is not so easy to give advice which is just and useful and the thought of the services you render to him ought not to prevent you from giving to God the tender affection which you owe him. This very tender love is so much more valuable.

Yes, all the more valuable; what is there in human nature so deeply rooted and so deeply adapted to it as its love for goodness? And is there any being other than God himself whose goodness is comparable to his? Is there any other good apart from God himself? What is more, in the presence of this goodness with its incomparable brilliance, splendour and beauty, the saintly soul is inflamed by the fire of love and cries out: "With all my being I thirst for God, the omnipotent, the living God: when will I come to see the face of God himself?"

17. I hope, dear brother, that you will not disdain this friendly criticism nor turn a deaf ear to the words of the Holy Spirit. I hope, beloved friend, that you will fulfil my desire and my long waiting so that my soul be freed from the anxieties, cares and the fears it suffers on your behalf. For if it happened to you—and may God preserve you from it—that you left this life before fulfilling your vow, you would leave me prey to constant sadness, a man without the hope of any consolation.

18. That is why I am so keen that you make the point of being kind enough to come to see me when on a pilgrimage, for example, to St. Nicholas. You will then meet up with the one who is more fond of you than anyone else. Together we shall then be able to discuss our affairs, the ways of our religious life and common interests. I have confidence in Our Lord that you will not regret having braved the fatigue of such a journey.

19. This letter is much longer than a normal letter: as I am not able to talk to you face to face, I have made up for this by writing more. Keep out of all danger, dear brother: don't forget my advice, and keep well. This is my most fervent wish. I beg you to send me a copy of the life of St. Remi, as it is impossible to find it down here.
Farewell.

Some Extracts from the Carthusian Statutes

On Silence and Solitude
This is holy ground, where, as a man with his friend, the Lord and his servant often speak together; there, is the faithful soul frequently

united to the Word of God; there, is the bride made one with her Spouse; there, earth is joined to heaven, the divine to the human. The journey, however, is long, and the way dry and barren, that must be traveled to attain the fount of water in the land of promise.

In cell the monk occupies himself usefully and in an orderly manner, reading, writing, reciting psalms, praying, meditating, contemplating, working. . . . He makes a practice of resorting from time to time, to a tranquil listening of the heart, that allows God to enter through all its doors and passages.

The fruit of silence is known only to those with experience . . . there is gradually born within us of our silence itself, something that will draw us on to still greater silence. . . . God has led us into solitude to speak to our heart. Let our hearts be a living altar from which there constantly ascends before God pure prayer, with which all our acts should be imbued. Love for our brethren shows itself first of all in respect for their solitude.

By our total surrender, we profess before the world and witness to the ultimate reality of God. Our God-given joy in loving and serving him exclusively proves to the world that his gifts are a reality which can replace most of the so-called necessities of worldly life. It proves that the spiritual life is an everyday reality.

They [the Brothers] imitate the hidden life of Jesus at Nazareth when carrying out the daily tasks of the house. They praise God by their work. The Fathers, by the very fact of faithful observance of solitude, impart to the Charterhouse its special character and they give spiritual aid to the Brothers from whom in turn they receive much. . . .

Whenever the Brothers are not occupied with the Divine Office in Church or with work in their Obediences, they always return to cell as to a very sure and tranquil haven. Here they remain quietly and without noise as far as possible and follow with faithfulness the Order of the day, doing everything in the presence of God and in the name of Our Lord Jesus Christ, through him giving thanks to God the Father. Here they occupy themselves usefully in reading or meditation, especially on sacred Scripture, the food of the soul, or, in the measure possible, they give themselves to prayer. . . .

Interior recollection during work will lead a brother to contemplation. To attain this recollection it is always permissible while working to have recourse to short and, so to speak, ejaculatory prayers and even sometimes to interrupt the work with brief prayer. . . .

The aim of a brother's life is above all else that he be united with Christ and that he may abide in his love. Hence, whether in the solitude of his cell or in the midst of his work, aided by the grace of his vocation, he should strive wholeheartedly and at all times to keep his mind on God.

THE LIFE OF ST. GILBERT

The Life of St. Gilbert, from *John Capgrave's Lives of St. Augustine and St. Gilbert of Sempringham, And a Sermon*, edited by J. J. Munro. London: The Early English Text Society, Oxford University Press, 1910. Translated into modern English by Daniel M. La Corte.

The following brief selection includes the history of the Order of Gilbertines, founded specifically for women contemplatives by Gilbert of Sempringham (ca. 1089–1189). The *Book of St. Gilbert*, composed by Ralph de Insula, the sacrist at Sempringham around 1202 at the request of Archbishop Hubert Walter, chronicles Gilbert's intentions in founding a monastery following the *Rule of Benedict* specifically for several women of Lincolnshire. The Austin friar of Lynn, John Capgrave, translated the story of the saint into English in the fourteenth-century vernacular. In this selection, I have rendered Gilbert's Life into contemporary English. The history of the Gilbertines begins in 1130 when they received the support of bishop Alexander of Lincoln for the establishment of a women's monastic community under Gilbert's guidance. This selection not only outlines Gilbert's original motivations, but also highlights the logistical solutions applied to the rapidly growing double monastery.

The Life of St. Gilbert by John Capgrave, Part I

Chapter IV. Gilbert's First Nuns
Then Gilbert thought, among other things, that virginity was a great estate, one of the greatest virtues that may please God, and that the fruit of virginity bears the greatest fruit allowed in heaven. For this reason, he first ordained that the seven maidens which were inflamed with the love of God by his teaching, be cloistered from the vanities of the world and serve our Lord in quiet contemplation.

Therefore, in the shadow of the walls of the Church of St. Andrew, he built them cells where they might pray and also have access both of saying and hearing all the divine services. After that he joined to their service other certain women, who did not know Latin, and men also who were converted to religion, but were not clerics (not ordained priests), these all were ordained to be in the service of the contemplative nuns. After doing this he ordained that certain clerics, men who knew Latin, to be bound to strict rules, that they should have the governance of the entire community. To all these he provided drink, clothes, and other necessities from his rents and from other lawfully gotten goods.

For their souls he also provided spiritual sustenance; for the women he gave the Rule of Saint Benedict, to the men, he gave the Rule of Saint Augustine. Taught by the Holy Spirit sent from heaven, he established certain customs besides these rules. Thus he created for them, laws mixed with such temperance that from among many kinds of people, many habits, and many degrees, he exhorted them in our Lord, that they should all have but one soul and heart fixed on God.

THE CISTERCIANS: EARLY CISTERCIAN DOCUMENTS

From *The Cistercians: Ideals and Reality*, translated by Louis J. Lekai, pp. 443–44, 445–46, 448–50. Kent, Ohio: Kent State University Press, 1977.

The Cistercian Order began as a group of reform-minded monks who sought to live a life more strictly in accord with the *Rule of St. Benedict*. In 1098 Robert of Molesme led twenty-one monks to the site of the "new monastery" called Cîteaux, a piece of land donated free from feudal obligations which would be the center of renewal of monastic life in the twelfth century. The re-interpretation of the *Rule of Benedict* motivated the Cistercians' adherence to a life based on simplicity and poverty, as witnessed by their architecture and simply adorned manuscripts, as well as their spirituality based on simplicity. The *Exordium Cistercii*, created around 1123, briefly highlights the founders' desire for a literal inter-pretation of the *Rule* and thus recounts their establishment of a "new monastery." The *Summa Cartae Caritatis*, written in 1119, is the basic constitution of the Order establishing a structure of governance and hierarchy for the rapidly growing order. Note the unanimity sought in customs, diet, dress, and liturgical practices, as well as the section on lay brothers. The lay brothers provided the heavy labor that allowed the choir monks to pursue a more contemplative life.

Exordium Cistercii

I. Departure of the Cistercian Monks from Molesme
        In the diocese of Langres there lay, as is well known, a monastery by the name of Molesme; it was of great renown and outstanding in reli-gious fervor. Within a short time of its foundation God in his goodness enriched it with the gift of his graces, raised it to honor with the pres-ence of distinguished men, and caused it to be as great in possessions as it was resplendent in virtues. But, because possessions and virtues are not usually steady companions, several members of that holy community,

men truly wise and filled with higher aspirations, decided to pursue heavenly studies rather than to be entangled in earthly affairs. Accordingly, these lovers of virtue soon came to think about that poverty which is fruitful to man. They realized that, although life in that place was a godly and upright life, they observed the Rule they had vowed to keep in a way short of their desire and intention. They spoke amongst themselves and asked one another how they were to fulfill the verse: "I will fulfill my vows to you, vows which I made with my own lips" (Ps. 65:13). What more needs to be said? After common deliberation, together with the father of that monastery, Robert of blessed memory, twenty-one monks went out to try to carry out jointly what they had conceived with one spirit. Eventually, after many labors and extreme difficulties, which all who wish to devote their life to Christ must endure, they reached their goal. They came to Cîteaux, which was then a place of horror, a vast wilderness. Realizing that the asperity of the place accorded well with the strict design they had already conceived (in their minds), the soldiers of Christ found the place, almost as though divinely prepared, to be as alluring as their design had been dear.

II. Beginnings of the Monastery of Cîteaux

Thus in the year 1098 of the Incarnation of Our Lord, supported with the counsel and strengthened with the authority of the venerable Hugh, archbishop of the church of Lyons, and at the time legate of the Apostolic See, and of the God-fearing man, Walter, bishop of Chalon, and of Odo, the illustrious duke of Burgundy, these men began to transform the solitude they had found into an abbey; abbot Robert received the care of the monks and the shepherd's staff from the bishop of the diocese; and under him the others vowed stability in that place. But, after a short time it happened that the same abbot Robert was reclaimed by the monks of Molesme, and was returned to Molesme on the order of Pope Urban II and with the permission and consent of Walter, bishop of Chalon. He was replaced by Alberic, a religious and holy man. For the sake of peace this wise agreement was made between the monasteries and confirmed by the pope: henceforth neither of them would (permanently) accept the other's monk without a proper recommendation. Through the solicitude and industry of its new father and with

God's generous assistance, the New Monastery thereafter advanced in holiness, excelled in fame, and witnessed the increase of its temporal goods. The man of God, Alberic, who successfully ran his race for nine years (Phil. 2:16), obtained the crown of eternity in the tenth year. He was succeeded by the lord Stephen, an Englishman by nationality, an ardent lover of and staunch champion of religious life, poverty and regular discipline. In his days the words of Scripture came true: "The eyes of the Lord are upon the just and His ears hear their prayer" (Ps. 33:16). The little flock voiced its one and only complaint: that it was small in number. As I said, the "poor of Christ" came to fear and to dread almost to the point of despair one thing alone: that they might not be able to leave behind heirs to their poverty. For their neighbors applauded their holy life but abhorred its austerity and thus kept from imitating the men whose fervor they approved. Yet God, who can easily make great things from small ones and many things from a few, beyond all expectation, so aroused the hearts of many to the imitation of these monks that in the cell where the novices are tested, thirty had come to live under the same discipline: clerics as well as laymen, even nobles and men of power in the eyes of the world. Upon this so sudden and happy heavenly visitation the barren one which had no offspring began, not without reason, to rejoice; "Once forsaken, she now came to have many sons" (Isa. 54:1). And God did not cease to multiply His people, and to increase their joy, so that within about twelve years the happy mother came to see twenty abbots, drawn from her own sons as well as from the sons of her sons, like olive branches around her table. Indeed she did not think it out of order to follow the example of the holy Father Benedict whose Rule she embraced. Hence, as soon as the new plantation began to produce offshoots, blessed Father Stephen in his watchful wisdom provided a document of admirable discretion; it served as a trimming knife which was to cut off the outgrowth of division which, if unchecked, could suffocate the fruit of mutual peace. Very appropriately, he wished the document to be called a Charter of Charity, for, clearly, its whole content so breathed love that almost nothing else is seen to be treated there than this: "Owe no man anything, but to love one another" (Rom. 13:8). This charter, arranged by the same father and confirmed by the aforementioned twenty abbots, was also approved by apostolic authority. It contains in greater detail those things which we have said: here, however, we shall restrict ourselves to a brief summary.

Summa Cartae Caritatis

III. General Statute Between Abbeys

According to the tenor of the Charter, it was established among all abbeys of the Cistercian Order that: Mother-abbeys may not exact any temporal goods from their daughter-abbeys. A Father-Abbot visiting the monastery of an abbot-son, shall not bless that one's novice as monk, nor shall he admit an outsider for permanent stay, nor lastly, decree or ordain anything in that place against the local abbot's will, except in what relates to the care of souls. If he finds anything contrary to the Rule or to the Order in that place, he may charitably correct it, with the counsel of the local abbot. But, if by chance the local abbot is absent, he shall correct whatever he finds amiss. The abbot-son yields his place to the Father-Abbot not only in the chapter room, but everywhere else in the monastery. However, the Father-Abbot shall eat with the brethren in the refectory, for the sake of discipline, except in the absence of the local abbot. All other visiting abbots of our Order shall do likewise. But if several abbots come and the local abbot is absent, their senior shall eat in the guesthouse. Further, every abbot shall visit the abbeys founded by his monastery with paternal solicitude at least once a year. Whenever an abbot-son visits his mother abbey, he shall be given due reverence as befits an abbot. He shall occupy the place of the abbot in everything pertaining to the Order, but only during the absence of the abbot of the mother-abbey. For, when that one is present, the abbot-son shall yield to him in all things, as to a father. Hence he shall not eat with the guests when the Father-Abbot is at home, but in the refectory with the brethren.

IV. The Annual Chapter of Abbots

The abbey of Cîteaux, the mother of all, wisely reserved to itself the prerogative that every abbot must visit it once a year at the same time, to meet one another, to tend to the affairs of the Order, to strengthen the peace and to preserve charity. At Cîteaux all shall reverently and humbly obey the lord Abbot of Cîteaux and that holy assembly when dealing with the correction of wrongs, and if they are accused, they shall seek pardon. Only abbots shall make accusations. The assembly also made this wise provision: should it come to pass that the extreme poverty of any one of the abbots become known to the assembly all shall provide for this brother's relief according to the dictates of charity and (each) in the measure allowed by his own situation. Only two reasons shall justify (an abbot's) absence from the annual chapter: illness of the body, or the blessing of a novice. An abbot, to whom one of these applies, shall send his prior as his representative. But if anyone shall ever presume to stay at home for any other reason, at the next chapter he shall seek pardon for his fault and offer satisfaction according to the judgment of the abbots. And this shall be held to be a lesser fault. . . .

IX. The Founding of New Abbeys

It has been decreed that all our monasteries must be dedicated to the Queen of Heaven and Earth. No monastery shall be constructed within cities, castles and manors. No abbot shall be sent to a new place without at least twelve monks and the following books: a psalter, a book of hymns, a book of collects, an antiphonary, a gradual, the Rule, a missal; and without the prior construction of such places as an oratory, a refectory, a dormitory, a guest-house, and a gate-keeper's cell, so that the monks may immediately serve God and live in religious discipline. No living quarters, only animal shelters, shall be constructed outside the gate of the monastery. Also, to preserve an indissoluble and lasting unity among our abbeys it has been established: first, that the Rule of blessed Father Benedict shall be interpreted and kept in one and the same way; secondly, that there shall be found the same liturgical books, the same food, the same clothing, and lastly, the same customs and usages in everything.

X. Which Books Must Not Be Dissimilar

The missal, Gospel Book, book of epistles, book of collects, gradual, antiphonary, book of hymns, psalter, lectionary, Rule and calendar of saints shall be used everywhere in one and the same way.

XI. On Clothing

Clothing shall be simple and inexpensive, without underclothes, as the Rule prescribes. But this also must be observed: the outer cowls shall not be flocked with pile on the outside; and the day-shoes shall be made of cowhide.

XII. On Food

In addition to what the Rule prescribes about the pound of bread, the measure of drink, and the number of dishes, this must also be observed: the bread must be coarse, that is, prepared with a sieve. Where wheat is scarce, however, rye may be used. This rule shall not apply to the sick; they, and also the guests for whom it has been prescribed, shall be served wastel-bread. To those who are bled, there shall be given a pound of white bread, once, during the bleeding.

XIII. No One May Eat Meat or (Food Prepared with) Lard in the Monastery

In the monastery cooked dishes must always and everywhere be prepared without meat or lard; an exception is made (only) for the brethren who are seriously ill and for our hired workers. . . .

XV. Where the Monk's Food Is to Come From

Food for the monks of our Order ought to come from manual labor, agriculture, and the raising of animals. Hence we may possess, for our own use, streams, woodlands, vineyards, meadows, lands far removed from the dwellings of seculars, and animals, except those which tend to foster curiosity and to show themselves off rather than serve a useful purpose, such as deer, cranes, and other animals of this kind. To raise, feed, and take care of animals we may keep granges, either in the neighborhood or at a greater distance. These are to be supervised and managed by the lay-brothers.

XVI. No Monk May Live Outside the Monastic Enclosure

A monk whose proper home, according to the Rule, ought to be the monastery, may go to a grange as often as he is sent, but on no account may he live there for any long period of time.

XVII. Women May Not Live in Our Houses

At any time whatsoever—be it a time for cultivating or preserving food, or a time for washing particular objects of the monastery when this is necessary, or lastly, a time of any need whatsoever—it is absolutely forbidden for us and our lay-brothers to live under the same roof with women.

XVIII. Women Shall Not Enter Within the Monastery Gate

Women shall not be received as guests within the courtyard of our granges, nor shall they enter within the gate of the monastery. . . .

XX. These Affairs Are to Be Managed by Lay-Brothers

As has been said, these affairs are to be managed by lay-brothers or by hired workers. As we do with monks, we take under our care lay-brothers with the license of the bishops, who are members of our family and helpers in our work. We hold them to be our brothers and, equally with our monks, sharers of our goods both spiritual and temporal. . . .

XXIII. What Incomes We Renounce

Our very name (of monks) and the constitution of our Order prohibit (the possession of) churches, altar revenues, burials, tithes from the labor or harvest of outsiders, manors, serfs, land-rents, oven and mill revenues, and all other incomes of the kind, as contrary to the purity of the monastic vocation.

THE MILITARY ORDERS: THE KNIGHTS TEMPLAR AND THE HOSPITALLERS

THE KNIGHTS TEMPLAR: THE PRIMITIVE RULE

From *The Rule of the Templars: The French Text of the Rule of the Order of the Knights Templar*, translated and introduced by J. M. Upton-Ward, pp. 19–38. Studies in the History of Medieval Religion, 6. Woodbridge, Suffolk, UK: The Boydell Press, 1992.

The foundation of the Knights Templar is placed around 1119/1120 with the purpose of protecting pilgrims from Moslem attacks as they traveled to Palestine and Holy places in Jerusalem. Hugues de Payens (ca. 1070–1136), the founder of the Knights Templar, vowed to protect these pilgrims by forming a religious community dedicated to such protection. King of Jerusalem, Baldwin II, gave the Knights a site on the former Jewish Temple, from which they took their name. They based their vows on the *Rule of St. Augustine* and vowed poverty, chastity, and obedience. By 1128, Hugues received a Rule from the Council of Troyes to govern the community, accepting the vows and habit of the Cistercians, adding a crusader's vow and red cross to their habit. The Knight's customs were based on the Cistercian customs since Bernard of Clairvaux assisted in re-writing the Templar's Rule.

129

Here Begins the Prologue to the *Rule of the Temple*

1. We speak firstly to all those who secretly despise their own will and desire with a pure heart to serve the sovereign king as a knight and with studious care desire to wear, and wear permanently, the very noble armor of obedience. And therefore we admonish you, you who until now have led the lives of secular knights, in which Jesus Christ was not the cause, but which you embraced for human favor only, to follow those whom God has chosen from the mass of perdition and whom he has ordered through his gracious mercy to defend the Holy Church, and that you hasten to join them forever.

2. Above all things, whosoever would be a knight of Christ, choosing such holy orders, you in your profession of faith must unite pure diligence and firm perseverance, which is so worthy and so holy, and is known to be so noble, that if it is preserved untainted forever, you will deserve to keep company with the martyrs who gave their souls for Jesus Christ. In this religious order has flourished and is revitalized the order of knighthood. This knighthood despised the love of justice that constitutes its duties and did not do what it should, that is defend the poor, widows, orphans and churches, but strove to plunder, despoil and kill. God works well with us and our savior Jesus Christ; He has sent his friends from the Holy City of Jerusalem to the marches of France and Burgundy, who for our salvation and the spread of the true faith do not cease to offer their souls to God, a welcome sacrifice. . . .

Here Begins the Rule of the Poor Knighthood of the Temple

9. You who renounce your own wills, and you others serving the sovereign king with horses and arms, for the salvation of your souls, for a fixed term, strive everywhere with pure desire to hear Matins and the entire service according to canonical law and the customs of the regular masters of the Holy City of Jerusalem. O you venerable brothers, similarly God is with you, if you promise to despise the deceitful world in perpetual love of God, and scorn the temptations of your body: sustained by the food of God and watered and instructed in the

commandments of Our Lord, at the end of the Divine Office, none should fear to go into battle if he henceforth wears the crown.

10. But if any brother is sent through the work of the house and of Christianity in the East—something we believe will happen often— and cannot hear the Divine Office, he should say instead of Matins thirteen Paternosters; seven for each hour and nine for Vespers. And together we all order him to do so. But those who are sent for such a reason and cannot come at the hours set to hear the Divine Office, if possible the set hours should not be omitted, in order to render to God his due. . . .

On the Communal Life

34. One reads in the Holy Scriptures: *Dividebatur singulis prout cuique opus erat.* That is to say that to each was given according to his need. For this reason we say that no one should be elevated among you, but all should take care of the sick; and he who is less ill should thank God and not be troubled; and let whoever is worse humble himself through his infirmity and not become proud through pity. In this way all members will live in peace. And we forbid anyone to embrace excessive abstinence; but firmly keep the communal life.

On the Master

35. The Master may give to whomsoever he pleases the horse and armor and whatever he likes of another brother, and the brother to whom the given thing belongs should not become vexed or angry: for be certain that if he becomes angry he will go against God.

On Giving Counsel

36. Let only those brothers whom the Master knows will give wise and beneficial advice be called to the council; for this we command, and by no means everyone should be chosen. For when it happens that they wish to treat serious matters like the giving of communal land, or to speak

of the affairs of the house, or receive a brother, then if the Master wishes, it is appropriate to assemble the entire congregation to hear the advice of the whole chapter; and what seems to the Master best and most beneficial, let him do it.

On Brothers Sent Overseas

37. Brothers who are sent throughout divers countries of the world should endeavor to keep the commandments of the Rule according to their ability and live without reproach with regard to meat and wine, etc. so that they may receive a good report from outsiders and not sully by deed or word the precepts of the Order, and so that they may set an example of good works and wisdom; above all so that those with whom they associate and those in whose inns they lodge may be bestowed with honor. And if possible, the house where they sleep and take lodging should not be without light at night, so that shadowy enemies may not lead them to wickedness, which God forbids them.

On Keeping the Peace

38. Each brother should ensure that he does not incite another brother to wrath or anger, for the sovereign mercy of God holds the strong and weak brother equal, in the name of charity.

How the Brothers Should Go About

39. In order to carry out their holy duties and gain the glory of the Lord's joy and to escape the fear of hell-fire, it is fitting that all brothers who are professed strictly obey their Master. For nothing is dearer to Jesus Christ than obedience. For as soon as something is commanded by the Master or by him to whom the Master has given the authority, it should be done without delay as though Christ himself had commanded it. For thus said Jesus Christ through the mouth of David, and it is true: *Ob auditu auris obedivit mihi.* That is to say: "He obeyed me as soon as he heard me."

40. For this reason we pray and firmly command the knight brothers who have abandoned their own wills and all the others who serve for a fixed term not to presume to go out into the town or city without the permission of the Master or of the one who is given that office; except at night to the Sepulchre and the places of prayer which lie within the walls of the city of Jerusalem.

41. There, brothers may go in pairs, but otherwise may not go out by day or night; and when they have stopped at an inn, neither brother nor squire nor sergeant may go to another's lodging to see or speak to him without permission, as is said above. We command by common consent that in this Order which is ruled by God, no brother should fight or rest according to his own will, but according to the orders of the Master, to whom all should submit, that they may follow this pronouncement of Jesus Christ who said: *Non veni facere voluntatem meam, sed ejus que misit me, patris.* That is to say: "I did not come to do my own will, but the will of my father who sent me."

THE HOSPITALLERS

The Rule, Statutes and Customs of the Hospitallers, 1099–1310, translated and introduced by Col. E. J. King. London: Methuen, 1934; reprinted Methuen, 1981.

After 1099 when the Crusaders captured Jerusalem, an Order following the *Rule of St. Augustine* dedicated to the care of the pilgrims was founded (ca. 1104). In the year 1113, the first papal privilege for the Hospital of St. John established a hospice for Latin pilgrims in Jerusalem. The Order of the Hospitallers provided food and shelter and some medical care for sick poor pilgrims of the Holy land. Over time the Hospitallers expanded their mission to include the protection of pilgrims on the pilgrimage routes throughout the Holy Land and then to the defense of the crusader states. The following selections include the Papal bull confirming the foundation of the Hospitallers, a section from the Rule from Raymond du Puy (1120–1160), and statutes from the records of the Order. Note that care of the sick and marginalized is central to the Order's mission.

Papal Bull Confirming the Foundation of the Order of Hospitallers

Dated 15th February, 1113

PASCHAL the Bishop, servant of the servants of God, to his venerable son Gerard, founder and Provost (prepositus) of the Xenodocheum of Jerusalem, and to his lawful successors forever.

A pious request and desire should meet with satisfaction and fulfilment. Forasmuch as of thine affection thou hast requested that the Xenodocheum, which thou hast founded in the City of Jerusalem, near to the Church of the Blessed John Baptist, should be supported by the Apostolic See, and fostered by the patronage of the Blessed Apostle Peter. We therefore, being much pleased with the piety and earnestness of thine hospital work (*hospitalitas*), do receive thy petition with paternal kindness, and we ordain by virtue of the present decree that that House of God the Xenodocheum shall always be under the guardianship of the Apostolic See, and the protection of Blessed Peter.

All things therefore that have been acquired for the said Xenodocheum, by thy solicitude and perseverance, for the support of pilgrims, and for the needs of the poor, whether in the Church in Jerusalem, or in the parishes of churches in the territory of other cities, or have been presented by faithful men, no matter who, or may be presented in the future by the Grace of God, or may happen to be acquired by other lawful means, and whatsoever things have been granted, by our venerable brethren the Bishops of the Church in Jerusalem, either to thee or to thy successors and to the brethren there occupied in the care of the pilgrims, we decree shall be held forever in peace and undiminished.

Moreover we ordain that the Tithes of your produce, wheresoever collected at your charge and by your labour, shall be held and possessed by your Xenodocheum, notwithstanding the opposition of the Bishops and of the episcopal officers.

The donations also, which pious Princes have made to the said Xenodocheum from taxes and other imposts, we decree shall be held confirmed.

And at thy death, who art now the overseer (provisor) and Provost of that place, no one shall be appointed there by subtlety or intrigue or violence, but only he whom the professed brethren there shall provide and elect in accordance with God's will.

Moreover all honours or possessions, which the said Xenodocheum at present holds either beyond or on this side of the sea, that is to say in Asia or in Europe, or those which in the future by the bounty of God it shall obtain, we confirm them to thee and to thy successors, who shall be devoting themselves to hospital work with piety and earnestness, and through you to the said Xenodocheum forever.

To this we further decree that it shall be lawful for no man whatsoever rashly to disturb the said Xenodocheum, or to carry off its possessions, or to retain those carried off, or to lessen them, or to harass it with vexatious annoyances. But let all its possessions be preserved undiminished for the sole use and enjoyment of those for whose maintenance and support they have been granted.

Moreover we decree that the Xenodochea or Ptochea 1 in the western parts at Bourg St. Gilles, Asti, Pisa, Bari, Otranto, Tarento and Messina, known by the name and style "of Jerusalem," shall remain as they are today under thy rule and disposition and those of thy successors forever.

If therefore in the future any person, either ecclesiastic or secular, knowing this chapter of our ordinances should rashly attempt to contravene them, and if after a second or third warning he shall not make satisfactory and suitable amends, let him be deprived of his dignity, power and honour, and let him know he stands accused before the tribunal of God for the iniquity that he has perpetrated, and let him be kept from the most Sacred Body and Blood of our God and Redeemer our Lord Jesus Christ, and at the Last Judgement let him undergo the severest punishment. But upon all those dealing justly towards the said place may the peace of our Lord Jesus Christ rest, that here they may receive the reward of good conduct, and before the Universal Judge may enjoy the blessings of everlasting peace. Amen.

II. *The Rule of Blessed Raymond du Puy, 1120–60*

This Is the Constitution Ordained by Brother Raymond. In the name of God, I Raymond Servant of Christ's poor and Warden of the Hospital of Jerusalem, with the counsel of all the Chapter, both clerical and lay brethren, have established these commandments in the House of the Hospital of Jerusalem.

1. How the Brethren Should Make Their Profession.
Firstly, I ordain that all the brethren, engaging in the service of the poor, should keep the three things with the aid of God, which they have promised to God: that is to say, chastity and obedience, which means whatever thing is commanded them by their masters, and to live without property of their own: because God will require these three things of them at the Last Judgment.

2. What the Brethren Should Claim as Their Due.
And let them not claim more as their due than bread and water and raiment, which things are promised to them. And their clothing should be

humble, because Our Lord's poor, whose servants we confess ourselves to be, go naked. And it is a thing wrong and improper for the servant that he should be proud, and his Lord should be humble.

3. Concerning the Conduct of the Brethren and the Service
of the Churches and the Reception of the Sick.
Moreover this is decreed that their conduct should be decorous in church, and that their conversation should be appropriate, that is to say, that the clerics, deacons and sub-deacons should serve the priest at the altar in white raiment, and if the thing shall be necessary another cleric should render this service, and there should be a light every day in the church, both by day and by night, and the priest should go in white raiment to visit the sick, bearing reverently the Body of Our Lord, and the deacon or the sub-deacon, or at least an acolyte should go before, bearing the lantern with a candle burning, and the sponge with the holy water.

4. How the Brethren Should Go Abroad and Behave.
Moreover, when the brethren shall go to cities and castles, let them not go alone but two or three together, and they shall not go there with those whom they would, but with those whom their Master shall order, and when they shall be come there where they would go, let them remain together as united in their conduct as in their dress. And let nothing be done in all their movements which might offend the eyes of anyone, but only that which reveals their holiness. Moreover, when they shall be in a church or in a house or in any other place where there are women, let them keep guard over their modesty, and let no women wash their heads or their feet, or make their beds. May Our Lord, who dwelleth among his saints, keep guard over them in this matter.

**III. Statutes of Fr. Roger Des Moulins 1177–87;
From the Chapter-general of 1181**

That the Churches Should Be Regulated with the Knowledge of the Prior.
In the name of the Father and of the Son and of the Holy Ghost. Amen.
In the year of the Incarnation of Our Lord 1181 in the month of March,

on the Sunday on which they chant *"Letare Jerusalem"* (i.e., March 22),
I Roger, servant of Christ's poor, in the presence of the clerical and lay
brethren seated around in Chapter-General, to the honor of God and
the glory of our Religion, and the support and benefit of the sick poor. . . .

The Confirmation by the Master Roger of the Things That the House
Should Do.
Let all the brethren of the House of the Hospital, both those present
and those to come, know that the good customs of the House of the
Hospital of Jerusalem are as follows:
1. Firstly the Holy House of the Hospital is accustomed to receive sick
men and women, and is accustomed to keep doctors who have the care
of the sick, and who make the syrups for the sick, and who provide the
things that are necessary for the sick. For three days in the week the
sick are accustomed to have fresh meat, either pork or mutton, and those
who are unable to eat it have chicken.
2. And two sick persons are accustomed to have one cloak of sheepskin
(*pelice de brebis*), which they use when going to the latrines (*chambres*),
and between two sick persons one pair of boots. Every year the House
of the Hospital is accustomed to give to the poor one thousand cloaks
of thick lamb skins.
3. And all the children abandoned by their fathers and mothers the
Hospital is accustomed to receive and to nourish. To a man and woman
who desire to enter into matrimony, and who possess nothing with
which to celebrate their marriage, the House of the Hospital is accustomed to give two bowls (*escueles*) or the rations of two brethren.
4. And the House of the Hospital is accustomed to keep one brother
shoemaker (*corvoisier*) and three sergeants, who repair the old shoes
(*soliers*) given for the love of God. And the Almoner is accustomed to
keep two sergeants who repair the old robes that he may give them to
the poor. . . .

THE MENDICANTS:
FRANCIS, CLARE, AND DOMINIC

INTRODUCTION TO SAINT FRANCIS, *THE RULE OF 1223* AND
THE FIRST RULE OF THE THIRD ORDER

From St. Francis of Assisi, *The Rule of 1223 and First Rule of the Third
Order*. In *The Writings of St. Francis of Assisi*, edited by Placid Herman.
London: Burns and Oates, 1964. Reprinted as part of *St. Francis of Assisi:
Writings and Early Biographies: English Omnibus of the Sources for the Life
of St. Francis*, 4th rev. ed., edited by Marion A. Habig, O.F.M. Quincy,
Ill.: Quincy College–Franciscan Press, 1991.

St. Francis of Assisi (1181–1226) is the author of *The Rule of 1223* and
The First Rule of the Third Order. The Rule of 1223 is for male Franciscans, the Friars Minor, members of the First Order.[1] The First Rule
of the Third Order is St. Francis's rule for lay secular members of his
order, both male and female; these are men and women who lead secular lives in their home communities but who take vows and who follow
the Rule of the Third Order especially written for them—they are Ter-
tiaries, members of the Third Order. The central biblical passages
behind Francis's mendicant ideal are the words of Jesus: "Jesus said to
him, 'If you wish to be perfect, go, sell your possessions, and give the
money to the poor, and you will have treasure in heaven; then come,

---

[1] *The Rule of St. Clare*, which follows, is for female Franciscans, the Poor
Clares, members of the Second Order. It was written by Clare, not Francis.

139

follow me'" (Matt. 19:21); "He said to them, 'Take nothing for your journey, no staff, nor bag, nor bread, nor money—not even an extra tunic . . .'" (Luke 9:3); "Then Jesus told his disciples, 'If any want to become my followers, let them deny themselves and take up their cross and follow me . . .'" (Matt. 16:24).

Selections from Saint Francis, *The Rule of 1223*

Chapter 1. In the name of the Lord begins the life of the Friars Minor.

The Rule and life of the Friars Minor is this, namely, to observe the Holy Gospel of our Lord Jesus Christ by living in obedience, without property, and in chastity. Brother Francis promises obedience and reverence to his holiness Pope Honorius and his lawfully elected successors and to the Church of Rome. The other friars are bound to obey Brother Francis and his successors.

Chapter 2. Of those who wish to take up this life and how they are to be received.

If anyone wants to profess our Rule and come to the friars, they must send him to their provincial minister, because he alone, to the exclusion of others, has permission to receive friars into the Order. The ministers must carefully examine all candidates on the Catholic faith and the sacraments of the Church. If they believe all that the Catholic faith teaches and are prepared to profess it loyally, holding by it steadfastly to the end of their lives, and if they are not married; or if they are married and their wives have already entered a convent or after taking a vow of chastity have by the authority of the bishop of the diocese been granted this permission; and the wives are of such an age that no suspicion can arise concerning them: let the ministers tell them what the holy Gospel says (Matt. 19:21), that they should go and sell all that belongs to them and endeavor to give it to the poor. If they cannot do this, their good will is sufficient.

The friars and their ministers must be careful not to become involved in the temporal affairs of newcomers to the Order, so that they may dispose of their goods freely, as God inspires them. If they ask for advice, the ministers may refer them to some God-fearing persons who can advise them how to distribute their property to the poor. When this has been done, the ministers should clothe the candidates with the habit of probation, namely, two tunics without a hood, a cord and trousers, and a caperon reaching to the cord, unless the ministers themselves at any time decide that something else is more suitable. After the year of the novitiate, they should be received to obedience, promising to live always according to this life and Rule. It is absolutely forbidden to leave the Order, as his holiness the Pope has laid down. For the Gospel tells us, "No one, having put his hand to the plough and looking back, is fit for the kingdom of God" (Luke 9:62).

The friars who have already vowed to obedience may have one tunic with a hood and those who wish may have another without a hood. Those who are forced by necessity may wear shoes. All the friars are to wear poor clothes and they can use pieces of sackcloth and other material to mend them, with God's blessing.

I warn all the friars and exhort them not to condemn or look down on people whom they see wearing soft or gaudy clothes and enjoying luxuries in food or drink; each one should rather condemn and despise himself. . . .

Chapter 4. The friars are forbidden to accept money.

I strictly forbid all the friars to accept money in any form, either personally or through an intermediary. The ministers and superiors, however, are bound to provide carefully for the needs of the sick and the clothing of the other friars, by having recourse to spiritual friends, while taking into account differences of place, season, or severe climate, as seems best to them in the circumstances. This does not dispense them from the prohibition of receiving money in any form.

Chapter 5. The manner of working.

The friars to whom God has given the grace of working should work in a spirit of faith and devotion and avoid idleness, which is the enemy of the soul, without however extinguishing the spirit of prayer and devotion, to which every temporal consideration must be subordinate. As wages for their labor they may accept anything necessary for their temporal needs, for themselves or their brethren, except money in any form. And they should accept it humbly as is expected of those who serve God and strive after the highest poverty. . . .

Chapter 11. The friars are forbidden to enter the monasteries of nuns.

I strictly forbid all the friars to have suspicious relationships or conversations with women. No one may enter the monasteries of nuns, except those who have received special permission from the Apostolic See. They are forbidden to be sponsors of men or women lest scandal arise amongst or concerning the friars.

Selections from Saint Francis, *The First Rule of the Third Order*

Here begins the Rule of the Continent Brothers and Sisters in the Name of the Father and of the Son and of the Holy Spirit. Amen.
The memorial of what is proposed for the Brothers and Sisters of Penance living in their own homes, begun in the year of our Lord 1221, is as follows.

Chapter I. Daily Life

1. The men belonging to this brotherhood shall dress in humble, undyed cloth, the price of which is not to exceed six Ravenna *soldi an ell*,[2] unless for evident and necessary cause a temporary dispensation be given. And breadth and thinness of the cloth are to be considered in said price.

2. They shall wear their outer garments and furred coats without open throat, sewed shut or uncut but certainly laced up, not open as secular people wear them; and they shall wear their sleeves closed.

3. The sisters in turn shall wear an outer garment and tunic made of cloth of the same price and humble quality; or at least they are to have with the outer garment a white or black underwrap or petticoat, or an ample linen gown without gathers, the price of an ell which is not to

---

[2]The smallest amount in the coin of the day for a forty-five inch length of cloth.

exceed twelve Pisa *denars*.[3] As to this price, however, and the fur cloaks they wear a dispensation may be given according to the estate of the woman and the custom of the place. They are not to wear silken or dyed veils and ribbons.

4. And both the brothers and the sisters shall have their fur garments of lamb's wool only. They are permitted to have leather purses and belts sewed in simple fashion without silken thread, and no other kind. Also other vain adornments they shall lay aside at the bidding of the Visitor.

5. They are not to go to unseemly parties or to shows or dances. They shall not donate to actors, and shall forbid their household to donate. . . .

Chapter VII. Visiting the Sick, Burying the Dead

22. Whenever any brother or sister happens to fall ill, the ministers, if the patient let them know of it, shall in person or through others visit the patient once a week, and remind him of penance; and if they find it expedient, they are to supply him from the common fund with what he may need for the body.

23. And if the ailing person depart from this life, it is to be published to the brothers and sisters who may be present in the city or place, so that they may gather for the funeral; and they are not to leave until the Mass has been celebrated and the body consigned to burial. Thereupon each member within eight days of the demise shall say for the soul of the deceased: a Mass, if he is a priest; fifty psalms, if he understands the Psalter, or if not, then fifty Our Fathers with the *Requiem aeternam* at the end of each.

24. In addition, every year, for the welfare of the brothers and sisters living and dead, each priest is to say three Masses, each member knowing the Psalter is to recite it, and the rest shall say one hundred Our Fathers with the *Requiem aeternam* at the end of each.

---

[3] A small amount; twelve pennies minted in Pisa.

25. All who have the right are to make their last will and make disposition of their goods within three months after their profession, lest anyone of them die intestate.

26. As regards making peace among the brothers and sisters or nonmembers at odds, let what the ministers find proper be done; even, if it be expedient, upon consultation with the Lord Bishop.

27. If contrary to their right and privileges trouble is made for the brothers and sisters by the mayors and governors of the places where they live, the ministers of the place shall do what they shall find expedient on the advice of the Lord Bishop.

28. Let each member accept and faithfully exercise the ministry of other offices imposed on him, although anyone may retire from office after a year.

29. When anybody wishes to enter this brotherhood, the ministers shall carefully inquire into his standing and occupation, and they shall explain to him the obligations of the brotherhood, especially that of restoring what belongs to others. And if he is content with it, let him be vested according to the prescribed way, and he must make satisfaction for his debts, paying money according to what pledged provision is given. They are to reconcile themselves with their neighbors and to pay up their tithes.

30. After these particulars are complied with, when the year is up and he seems suitable to them, let him on the advice of some discreet brothers be received on this condition: that he promise he will all the time of his life observe everything here written, or to be written or abated on the advice of the brothers, unless on occasion there be a valid dispensation by the ministers; and that he will, when called upon by the ministers, render satisfaction as the Visitor shall ordain if he have done anything contrary to this condition. And this promise is to be put in writing then and there by a public notary. Even so nobody is to be received otherwise, unless in consideration of the estate and rank of the person it shall seem advisable to the ministers.

31. No one is to depart from this brotherhood and from what is contained herein, except to enter a religious Order.

32. No heretic or person in bad repute for heresy is to be received. If he is under suspicion of it, he may be admitted if otherwise fit, upon being cleared before the bishop.

33. Married women are not to be received except with the consent and leave of their husbands.

34. Brothers and Sisters ejected from the brotherhood as incorrigible are not to be received in it again except it please the saner portion of the brothers.

Chapter VIII. Correction, Dispensation, Officers

35. The ministers of any city or place shall report public faults of the brothers and sisters to the Visitor for punishment. And if anyone proves incorrigible, after consultation with some of the discreet brothers he should be denounced to the Visitor, to be expelled by him from the brotherhood, and thereupon it should be published in the meeting. Moreover, if it is a brother, he should be denounced to the mayor or the governor.

36. If anyone learns that scandal is occurring relative to brothers and sisters, he shall report it to the ministers and shall have opportunity to report it to the Visitor. He need not be held to report it in the case of husband against wife.

37. The Visitor has the power to dispense all the brothers and sisters in any of these points if he finds it advisable.

38. When the year has passed, the ministers with the counsel of the brothers are to elect two other ministers; and a faithful treasurer, who is to provide for the need of the brothers and sisters and other poor; and messengers who at the command of the ministers are to publish what is said and done by the fraternity.

39. In all the above mentioned points no one is to be obligated under guilt, but under penalty; yet so that if after being admonished twice by the ministers he should fail to discharge the penalty imposed or to be imposed on him by the Visitor, he shall be obligated under guilt as contumacious.

INTRODUCTION TO SAINT CLARE OF ASSISI,
THE RULE OF ST. CLARE

From St. Clare of Assisi, *The Rule of Saint Clare*. In *Rule and Testament of St. Clare: Constitutions for Poor Clare Nuns*, translated by Mother Mary Francis. Chicago: Franciscan Herald Press, 1987.

Saint Clare of Assisi (1194–1253) wrote the Rule of St. Clare for nuns and sisters who wished to share in the religious life developed by St. Francis. After much work, Clare's Rule was approved by Pope Innocent IV on August 9, 1253. These women lived in a cloister like Benedictine and all other nuns; they did not go out into the world as the Friars did to beg, to preach, to teach, or to do good works. Though the sisters lived entirely within the cloister, the sisters could leave to do gardening and other work related to the monastery. Franciscan nuns, unlike earlier nuns, strove for absolute poverty, both personal and corporate, calling themselves the Poor Clares, and following the teachings of St. Francis.

Chapter I. In The Name of the Lord Begins the Form of Life of the Poor Sisters

The form of life of the Order of the Poor Sisters which the blessed Francis founded is this: to observe the holy Gospel of our Lord Jesus Christ, by living by obedience, without anything of one's own, and in chastity. Clare, unworthy handmaid of Christ and little plant of the most blessed Father Francis, promises obedience and reverence to the Lord Pope Innocent and to his successors canonically elected, and to the Roman Church. And just as in the beginning of her own conversion, she together with her Sisters promised obedience to the blessed Francis, even so does she promise to preserve the same inviolably to his successors. And the other Sisters shall always be bound to obey the successors of the blessed Francis, and so, too, Sister Clare and the other Abbesses canonically elected who shall succeed her.

Chapter II. Those Who Desire to Embrace This Life and How They Are to be Received

If, by divine inspiration, anyone should come to us desiring to embrace this life, the Abbess is bound to seek the consent of all the Sisters; and if the greater part shall have been in agreement, she may receive her, having had the permission of our Lord Cardinal Protector. And if she judges her acceptable, let the Abbess carefully examine her or have her examined concerning the Catholic faith and the sacraments of the Church. And if she believes all these things and is willing to confess them faithfully and to observe them steadfastly to the end, and if she has no husband (or, if she does have, he has already entered religious life with the authority of the Bishop of the diocese and already made a vow of continence), and if there is no impediment to the observance of this life such as advanced age or ill-heath or mental weakness, let the tenor of our life be thoroughly explained to her.

And if she be suitable, let the words of the holy Gospel be addressed to her: that she should go and sell all that she has and take care to distribute the proceeds to the poor. But if she cannot do this, her good will suffices. And let the Abbess and her Sisters be on their guard not to be anxious about her temporal affairs, so that she may freely do with her possessions whatsoever the Lord may inspire her. If, however, some advice would be needed, let them send her to some discerning and God-fearing men by whose counsel let her goods be distributed to the poor.

Afterwards, her hair having been cut off round and her secular dress laid aside, she is to be allowed three tunics and a mantle.

From then on, it shall not be permitted her to go outside the monastery except for a useful, reasonable, clear and approved cause.

When the year of probation is ended, she may be received to obedience, promising to observe perpetually our life and form of poverty.

No one may be veiled during the time of probation. The Sisters may also have little mantles for the convenience and propriety of their service and labor. Indeed, the Abbess should with good judgment provide them with garments according to the difference of persons and according to places and seasons and cold climates as she may deem it of necessity right to do.

Young girls received into the monastery before the age required by law shall have their hair cut off round and, their secular dress being laid aside, shall be clothed in religious garb as it shall seem fitting to the Abbess. But when they have reached the age required by law, they shall make their profession clothed after the manner of the others.

And for these as well as for the other novices, the Abbess must solicitously provide a Mistress from among all the more discerning of the monastery who shall devotedly form them in holy living and becoming behavior according to the form of our profession.

The same form as above shall be observed in the examination and reception of the Sisters serving outside the monastery: they may wear shoes.

No one may live with us in the monastery unless she has been received according to the form of our profession.

And for the love of the most holy and most beloved Child wrapped in such poor little swaddling clothes and laid in a manger, and of his most holy Mother, I direct, pray and exhort my Sisters that they be always clothed in the garments of the lowly.

Chapter V. Silence, the Parlor and the Grille

The Sisters must keep silence from the hour of Compline until Terce, except those serving outside the monastery. Let them also be silent continually in the church, in the dormitory, in the refectory only while they are eating; in the infirmary, however, it is permitted the Sisters always to speak discreetly in what concerns the recreation and service of the sick. Nevertheless, they may always and everywhere communicate what is necessary in a subdued tone of voice.

It is not allowed the Sisters to speak in the parlor or at the grille without permission of the Abbess or her Vicaress. And those who have permission to speak in the parlor should not dare do so except in the presence and hearing of two Sisters. Moreover, they may not presume to go to the grille unless there are present at least three Sisters assigned by the Abbess or her Vicaress from those eight Discreets who have been elected from among all the Sisters for the council of the Abbess. The Abbess and her Vicaress are themselves bound to observe this manner of speaking. And what is more, speaking very rarely at the grille, but at the door it may never be at all.

There is to be attached to the grille on the inside a curtain which may not be removed unless the word of God is being preached or if a Sister would be speaking to someone. It should also have a wooden door, well fastened with two distinct iron locks, bolts and bars, which must be locked especially at night with two keys of which the Abbess shall have one and the sacristan the other. And it must always remain locked except when the Divine Office is being prayed and for the reasons mentioned above.

No Sister may under any circumstance speak at the grille to anyone before sunrise or after sunset.

Moreover, at the parlor on the inside there must always be a curtain which is not to be removed.

During the Lent of Saint Martin and the greater Lent, no one may speak in the parlor except to the priest in the case of confession or some other manifest necessity which must be reserved to the prudence of the Abbess or her Vicaress.

Chapter XI: The Keeping of the Enclosure

The portress, who should be mature in her manner of acting and discreet and of a suitable age, shall remain stationed during the day in an open cell without a door. And let some well-qualified companion be assigned to her who may take her place in all things whenever necessary.

Moreover, the door should be secured as strongly as possible with two different iron locks, bars and bolts so that, more especially at night, it may be locked with two keys, one of which the Sister in charge of the door shall have, the Abbess the other. And during the day it may by no means be left without a custodian but should be securely locked with one key.

Again, let them most diligently take care and make sure that the door never stands open unless this could hardly be avoided gracefully. Neither may it be opened under any circumstance to anyone wishing to enter except to one who will have been given permission by the Supreme Pontiff or by our Lord Cardinal. Nor may the Sisters allow anyone to enter the monastery before sunrise or to remain inside after sunset except for a clear, reasonable and unavoidable cause demanding it.

If permission will have been given for any Bishop to celebrate Mass inside for the blessing of an Abbess or for the consecration of any of the Sisters as a nun or yet again for some other reason, let him be satisfied with as few and as suitable companions and assistants as possible.

Whenever it shall be necessary for others to enter inside the monastery for doing work, then let the Abbess solicitously place a suitable person at the door who shall open it only to those designated for the work and to no others.

Let all the Sisters most earnestly then take care that they not be seen by those entering.

THE DOMINICAN FRIARS

In 1216, the Dominicans, called the Order of Preachers (from the Latin *Ordo Praedicatorum*), were officially recognized. The order follows the *Rule of Saint Augustine* and adapted the flexible *Regula* to their mission as preachers. Responding to the twelfth-century notion of the apostolic life, Dominic (1170–1221) insisted on absolute poverty for his Order, much like the Franciscans. Unlike the Franciscans the Dominicans were well trained in theology and would establish schools, at first to educate their brethren. Initially, these highly educated preachers responded to the Albigensian heresies in Southern France, and later produced the greatest philosophers and theologians in Western Christendom. In this selection, Blessed Jordan of Saxony (ca. 1190–1237) provides a first-hand account to the foundation and early history of the Dominicans. His *Libellus*, written sometime during 1233, most likely as an encyclical letter to the entire Order soon after the canonization of the Founder, provides a chronicle not only of the life of Dominic but also the early period of the Order of Dominicans.

The Dominican Order and Way of Life

The following selections come from *Saint Dominic: Biographical Documents*, edited with an introduction by Francis C. Lehner, O.P., foreword by Most Reverend Aniceto Fernandez, O.P. Washington, D.C.: Thomist Press, 1964.

How Master Dominic Went to the Pope
With the Bishop of Toulouse

40. This same bishop took Brother Dominic as his companion to the council and, together, they besought the Lord Pope Innocent to confirm Brother Dominic and his companions in an Order which would be called and would be an Order of Preachers, as well as to ratify the revenues already assigned to the brethren by the Count and the Bishop.

41. After listening to this request, the head of the Roman See urged Brother Dominic to return to his brethren and, after a full discussion with them on the matter of unanimously accepting an already approved rule, the Bishop should assign them a church. After that, he was to return and get the Pope's approval of their work.

42. Accordingly, after the council, Dominic returned to Toulouse and, calling the brethren together, he notified them of the Lord Pope's wishes. Now the future preachers chose the Rule of St. Augustine, who had been an outstanding preacher, and added to it some stricter details about food and fasts, as well as about bedding and clothing. They agreed, also, to hold no possessions, lest concern about temporal things be an obstacle to their office of preaching, but would remain content with their revenue.

43. Along with this, the Bishop of Toulouse, with the consent of his chapter, assigned them three churches: one within the city, another in the village of Parniers, and a third between Sorèze and Puylaurens, called the Church of St. Mary of Lescure. A convent and priory were to be attached to each of these churches.

The First Church Conferred on the Brethren at Toulouse

44. During the summer of 1216 the brethren received the first church in the city of Toulouse, which had been built in honor of St. Romain. None of the brethren had ever lived in either of the other two churches. But in the church of St. Romain they built an enclosure, above which were cells for study and sleep. At that time the brethren numbered about sixteen. . . .

Death of Lord Innocent and Elevation of Pope Honorius, Who Confirmed the Order

45. In the meantime, the Lord Pope Innocent died and was succeeded by Honorius, upon whom Dominic called at once in order to present the plan and organization agreed upon for his Order. From him he

obtained full and complete confirmation of the Order and of everything else he requested.

The Vision (Dominic) Saw at Rome in the Basilica of the Apostles Peter and Paul. Once when the servant of God, Dominic, was at
Rome in the Basilica of St. Peter, where he was praying fervently in
God's sight for the preservation and growth of his Order, which the right
hand of God had raised up through him, he saw the glorious princes,
Peter and Paul, coming toward him in a sudden vision wrought by the
power of God. Peter, who was first, seemed to be handing him a staff,
and Paul a book. Then they spoke these words: "Go and preach, because
you have been chosen by God for this work." And then, in a moment
of time, he seemed to see all his children dispersed through the world
and going two by two preaching the word of God to the people.

When the Order should have been confirmed by the Apostolic (successor), he commanded the secretary to put down "Preaching Friars"
in addressing the Order. Writing the letter of confirmation, (the secretary) directly put down "Friars Preachers." When he looked at the
letter, the Apostolic (successor) asked the secretary, "Why have you
not written 'Preaching Friars,' as I told you? Did you want to write
'Preachers'?" In all calmness, the latter answered, "'Preaching' is an
adjective, although it may be granted that a participle can be used as a
substantive and serve as a common noun denoting an act; but 'Preachers' is properly a substantive, and is both a verbal and personal noun
wherein the name of the function is most clearly stated." You see, then,
reader, how truly the secretary answered the objections. For "preaching" never signifies its content other than by way of an act, whereas
"preacher" signifies its content after the manner of a habit, even though
(this content) may not always be an act; and therefore it was fitting
that "preacher" be put down. The Apostolic Lord (Pope) agreeing with
(this) most patent argument, the Order received the title of Preachers
and was solemnly confirmed by the cardinals. The Lateran Council
having been celebrated in the year of our Lord 1215, the Pope, ordering certain agenda pertinent to the promotion of the faith in the Toulouse
area, and deciding to write about these agenda to Blessed Dominic
and those who were with him, told a secretary whom he had called,
"Sit down and write about these matters to 'Brother Dominic and his

Companions' in (exactly) these words." And after standing up a bit, he said, "Do not write it that way, but in this manner: 'Brother Dominic and Those Who Are Preaching With Him in the Area of Toulouse', etc." And immediately after taking more time for further consideration, he said, "Put it down this way: 'Master Dominic and the Friars Preachers, etc.'" and he got up. This is how the Lord (Pope) said it, and this is how the secretary wrote it.

Honorius III Confirms the Order

Honorius, bishop, servant of the servants of God, to the beloved sons Dominic, prior of St. Romanus in Toulouse, and his brethren, both present and future, professed in the regular life. *In perpetuum.*

It is fitting that apostolic protection should be extended to those choosing the religious life, lest temerarious attacks should possibly turn them away from their purpose or, God forbid, destroy the vigor of the sacred religious institute. Wherefore, beloved sons in the Lord, we benevolently assent to your just requests. We take the Church of St. Romanus in Toulouse, where you have given yourselves to the service of God, under the protection of St. Peter and our own, and we secure it with the present written privilege.

In the first place, indeed, we decree that the canonical Order which is known to be established according to God and the Rule of St. Augustine in the said Church should be inviolably preserved forever.

Moreover, that whatever possessions and whatever goods the said church at present justly and canonically possesses or shall be able, the Lord granting, to acquire in the future through the concession of the popes, the liberality of kings or princes, the offerings of the faithful, or other just means, should belong firmly and inviolably to you and your successors. Among these goods, we have deemed it well to name the following: the place itself where the said church is situated, with its properties; the church of Prouille with its properties; the estate of Caussanel with its properties; the church of St. Mary of Lescure with its properties; the hospice in Toulouse, called "the Hospice of Arnold Bernard," with its properties; the church of the Holy Trinity in Loubens, with its properties; and the tithes which, in his good and provident liberality, our venerable brother Foulques, the bishop of Toulouse, with the consent of his chapter, has given you, as this is more explicitly contained in his letters.

Also let no one presume to exact or extort from you tithes from the fruits of the lands which you cultivate with your own hands or at your own expense, or from the produce of your animals.

Moreover, you may receive and keep, without opposition from anyone, members of the clergy or the laity who are free men and unencumbered by debt, who flee from the world to enter the religious life.

Furthermore, we prohibit any of your brethren, after they have made profession in your church to depart from it without the permission of their prior, except for the purpose of entering a stricter religious institute. If one should leave, let no one dare to receive him without the authorization of a letter from your community.

In the parochial churches which you hold, you may select priests and present them to the bishop of the diocese, to whom, if they are worthy, the bishop shall entrust the care of souls, so that they may be responsible to him in spiritual matters and to you in temporal matters.

We decree further that no one may impose new and unjust exactions on your church, or promulgate sentences of excommunication or interdict on you or your church without a manifest and just cause. When, however, a general interdict shall be laid on the whole territory, it will be permitted to you to celebrate the Divine Office behind closed doors, chanting in a low voice, not ringing the bells, and excluding those under excommunication and interdict.

The sacred Chrism, holy oils, the consecration of altars or basilicas, and the ordination of clerics who are to be promoted to holy orders, you shall obtain from the bishop of the diocese, so long as he is a Catholic and in grace and communion with the most holy Roman See and is willing to impart these to you without any irregularity. Otherwise, you may approach any Catholic bishop you may choose, provided he be in grace and communion with the Apostolic See; and armed with our authority, he may impart to you what you petition.

Moreover, we grant this place freedom of burial. Let no one, then, place an obstacle to the devotion and last will of those who choose to be buried there, provided they are not excommunicated or under interdict. However, the just rights of the churches from which the corpses are taken must be safeguarded.

When you, who are now the Prior of this place, or any of your successors shall go out of office, no one shall be appointed by secret craftiness or violence; but only he whom the brethren, by common agreement, or whom those brethren who are of more mature and sound judgment shall choose to elect according to God and the Rule of St. Augustine.

Furthermore, the liberties, ancient immunities, and reasonable customs granted to your church and observed up to this time, we ratify and command that they shall endure inviolably for all future time. We decree, therefore, that no one may rashly disturb the aforementioned church, take away its possessions or, having removed, keep them, diminish them, or harass them by any kind of molestation, but all these goods shall be preserved intact entirely for the control, sustenance, and use of those for whom they have been granted, saving the authority of the Apostolic See and the canonical rights of the diocesan bishop.

If, therefore, in the future any ecclesiastical or secular person whosoever, having knowledge of this our document, shall rashly attempt to contravene it, and if, after a second or third admonition, he refuses to correct his fault by fitting satisfaction, let him forfeit the dignity of his power and honor; and let him know that he shall stand guilty of the perpetrated evil before God's judgment and shall be denied the most sacred Body and Blood of our God and Lord, our Savior Jesus Christ, and shall, at the last judgment, be delivered to strict vengeance. Nevertheless, may all those who uphold the rights of the said place have the peace of Our Lord Jesus Christ, receive the fruit of good action here on earth, and, before the Just Judge, receive the rewards of eternal peace. Amen, amen, amen.

I, Honorius, Bishop of the Catholic Church.
Perfect my steps in your ways. Fare ye well!
(Then follow the signatures of eighteen cardinals.)
Given at Rome at St. Peter, by the hand of Ranerio, Prior of Santo Fridiano in Lucca, Vice-Chancellor of the holy Roman Church, on the eleventh of the kalends of January, the fifth indiction, the 1216th year of Our Lord's Incarnation, the first year of the Lord Pope, Honorius III.

SELECTED BIBLIOGRAPHY

PRIMARY SOURCES

Ardo. *The Emperor's Monk: Contemporary Life of Benedict of Aniane.* Trans. Allen Cabaniss. Ilfracombe, Devon: A. H. Stockwell, 1979.

Athanasius. *The Life of Antony and the Letter to Marcellinus.* Trans. Robert C. Gregg. New York: Paulist Press, 1980.

Anthony, St. *The Letters of St. Antony the Great.* Trans. Derwas J. Chitty. Fairacres, Oxford: S.L.G. Press, 1975; reprint 1977.

Augustine, St. *The Rule of Our Holy Father St. Augustine: Bishop of Hippo.* Trans. Robert Russell. Villanova, Penn.: Province of St. Thomas of Villanova, 1976.

Basil, St. *The Long Rules.* Trans. M. Monica Wagner. Vol. 9 of *The Fathers of the Church: A New Translation.* Washington, D.C.: Catholic University of America Press, 1950; reprints 1962, 1970.

Benedict of Nursia, St. *RB 1980: The Rule of St. Benedict in English.* Ed. Timothy Fry. Collegeville, Minn.: The Liturgical Press, 1982.

Caesarius of Arles, St. *The Rule for Nuns of St. Caesarius of Arles.* Trans. and ed. Mother Maria Caritas McCarthy. Studies in Mediaeval History, n.s. 16. Washington, D.C.: Catholic University of America Press, 1960.

Cassian, John. *The Conferences.* Trans. Boniface Ramsey. Ancient Christian Writers: The Works of the Fathers in Translation, 57. New York: Paulist Press, 1997.

159

Clare of Assisi, St. "The Rule of Saint Clare." In *Rule and Testament of St. Clare: Constitutions for Poor Clare Nuns*, trans. Mary Francis, pp. 1–30. Chicago: Franciscan Herald Press, 1987.

Columbanus, St. "Rule for Monks by Columbanus." In *Sancti Columbani Opera*, ed. G. S. M. Walker, pp. 123–29, 135–41, 143. Shannon, Ireland: Irish University Press, 1957; reprint 1970.

Dominic, St. *Saint Dominic: Biographical Documents*. Ed. Francis C. Lehner. Washington, D.C.: Thomist Press: 1964.

Francis of Assisi, St. "The Rule of 1223" and "The First Rule of the Third Order." In *The Writings of St. Francis of Assisi*, ed. Placid Hermann, pp. 57–64, 168–78. London: Burns and Oates, 1964. Reprinted as part of *St. Francis of Assisi: Writings and Early Biographies: English Omnibus of the Sources for the Life of St. Francis*, 4th rev. ed., ed. Marion A. Habig. Quincy, Ill.: Quincy College-Franciscan Press, 1991.

King, Colonel E. J., trans. *The Rule, Statutes, and Customs of the Hospitallers, 1099–1310*. London: Methuen, 1934; reprint 1981.

Lekai, Louis Julius. *The Cistercians: Ideals and Reality*, esp. 442–50 for the translations of *The Exordium Cistercii* and *Summa Cartae Caritatis*. [Kent, Ohio]: Kent State University Press, 1977.

Lockhart, Robin Bruce. *Listening to Silence: An Anthology of Carthusian Writings*. London: Darton, Longman, & Todd, 1997.

The Master. *The Rule of the Master*. Trans. Luke Eberle; introd. by Adalbert de Vogüé and trans. Charles Philippi. Cistercian Studies 6. Kalamazoo, Mich.: Cistercian Publications, 1977.

Munro, J. J., ed. *John Capgrave's Lives of St. Augustine and St. Gilbert of Sempringham, and a Sermon*. London: The Early English Text Society, Oxford University Press, 1910.

Pachomius, St. *Pachomian Koinonia: The Lives, Rules and Other Writings of Saint Pachomius and His Disciples*. Trans. Armand Veilleux. 3 vols. Kalamazoo, Mich.: Cistercian Publications, 1980.

Pseudo-Athanasius. *The Life and Regimen of the Blessed and Holy Syncletica*. Trans. Elizabeth Bryson Bongie. Toronto: Peregrina, 2001.

Upton-Ward, J. M., trans. *The Rule of the Templars: The French Text of the Rule of the Order of the Knights Templar*. Studies in the History of Medieval Religion 4. Woodbridge, Suffolk, UK: Boydell Press, 1992.

Waldebert. *The Rule of a Certain Father to the Virgins*. Trans. Jo Ann McNamara and John Halborg. 2nd ed. Toronto: Peregrina, 1993.

William of Aquitaine. "The Foundation Charter of the Order of Cluny." In *Select Historical Documents of the Middle Ages*, pp. 329–33. Trans. and ed. Ernest F. Henderson. London: Bell and Sons, 1892.

ADDITIONAL SOURCES AND TRANSLATIONS

Ancren riwle. *The English Text of the Ancrene Riwle: The 'Vernon' Text*. Trans. Arne Zettersten and Bernhard Diensberg. Early English Text Society 310. Oxford: Oxford University Press, 2000.

Armstrong, Regis J., ed. and trans. *Clare of Assisi: Early Documents*. New York: Paulist Press, 1988.

Armstrong, Regis J., J. A. Wayne Hellmann, and William J. Short, eds. *Francis of Assisi: Early Documents*. 4 vols. Hyde Park, N.Y.: New City Press, 1999–2002.

Franklin, Carmela Vircillo, Ivan Havener, and J. Alcuin Francis, trans. *Early Monastic Rules: The Rules of the Fathers and the Regula Orientalis*. Collegeville, Minn.: The Liturgical Press, 1982.

Hildegard of Bingen. *An Explanation of the Athanasian Creed*. Trans. Thomas M. Izbicki. Toronto: Peregrina Publishing, 2001.

———. *Explanation of the Rule of Benedict*. Trans. Hugh Feiss. Toronto: Peregrina, 1998.

Ó Maidín, Uinseann. *The Celtic Monk: Rules and Writings of Early Irish Monks*. Kalamazoo, Mich.: Cistercian Publications, 1996.

Smith, Julie Ann. *Ordering Women's Lives: Penitentials and Nunnery Rules in the Early Medieval West*. Aldershot, England: Ashgate, 2001.

Swan, Laura. *The Forgotten Desert Mothers: Sayings, Lives, and Stories of Early Christian Women*. New York: Paulist Press, 2001.

Tugwell, Simon, ed. *Early Dominicans: Selected Writings*. New York: Paulist Press, 1982.

FURTHER READING

The best general survey on monastic history is C. H. Lawrence, *Medieval Monasticism: Forms of Religious Life in Western Europe in the Middle Ages*, third ed. (Harlow, England; New York: Longman, 2001). Lawrence's text would be a fine textbook companion to the primary sources above.

Studies on the specific Rules should include, for Saint Benedict's Rule, Adalbert de Vogüé's *Community and Abbot in the Rule of St. Benedict*, Cistercian Studies 5, vols. 1 and 2 (Kalamazoo, Mich.: Cistercian Publications, 1979, 1988). Saint Augustine's Rule is considered in George Lawless's *Augustine of Hippo and His Monastic Rule* (Oxford: Oxford University Press; New York: Clarendon Press, 1987). For work on Saint Basil's Rule one might consider Augustine Holmes, *A Life Pleasing to God: The Spirituality of the Rules of St Basil* (Kalamazoo, Mich.: Cistercian Publications, 2000).

On specific Orders, the following texts are recommended:

For Cluny, see Barbara H. Rosenwein, *Rhinoceros Bound: Cluny in the Tenth Century* (Philadelphia: University of Pennsylvania Press, 1982).

The life of Carthusian monks is outlined in Robin Bruce Lockhart, *Halfway to Heaven: The Hidden Life of the Carthusians* (Kalamazoo, Mich.: Cistercian Publications, 1999).

For the Gilbertines, the two following excellent studies are available: Sharon K. Elkins, *Holy Women of Twelfth-century England* (Chapel Hill: University of North Carolina Press, 1988); and Brian Golding, *Gilbert of Sempringham and the Gilbertine Order, c. 1130–c. 1300* (Oxford: Oxford University Press; New York: Clarendon Press, 1995).

The unofficial history of the Cistercian way of life can be found in Louis J. Lekai, *The Cistercians: Ideals and Reality* ([Kent], Ohio: Kent State University Press, 1977). A fine study on the intellectual history and spirituality of the Cistercians comes from John R. Sommerfeldt: his *The Spiritual Teachings of Bernard of Clairvaux: An Intellectual History of the Early Cistercian Order* (Kalamazoo, Mich.: Cistercian Publications, 1991) draws on primary sources to elucidate this Cistercian father's thought.

For the military orders, there is no better study than Dominic Selwood's *Knights of the Cloister: Templars and Hospitallers in Central-Southern Occitania, c. 1100–c. 1300* (Woodbridge, Suffolk: Boydell Press, 1999).

For further reading on the Friars one should consult the dated but still excellent study of the Franciscans by John R. H. Moorman, *A History of the Franciscan Order from its Origins to the Year 1517* (Oxford: Clarendon Press, 1968); and the authority on the history of Dominicans and their contributions to the religious life by William A. Hinnebusch, *The Dominicans: A Short History* (Dublin: Dominican Publications, 1985). For a more detailed analysis of the monastic approach to life, see the well respected work of Jean Leclercq, especially his *The Love of Learning and the Desire for God: A Study of Monastic Culture*, translated by Catharine Misrahi (New York: Fordham University Press, 1982). Highly recommended in the area of spirituality and prayer lives of monastics and religious is Bernard McGinn's multi-volume study on Mysticism in the Christian West: *The Presence of God: A History of Western Christian Mysticism*, vols. 1–3 (New York: Crossroad, 1991–1998). Additionally, religious life in the medieval period is well documented and analyzed by Giles Constable in his *The Reformation of the Twelfth Century* (Cambridge: Cambridge University Press, 1996), and especially in his *Three Studies in Medieval Religious and Social Thought* (Cambridge: Cambridge University Press, 1995). For a more detailed bibliography for the medieval period see Giles Constable's *Medieval Monasticism: A Select Bibliography* (Toronto: University of Toronto Press, 1976).

In recent years, much work has been done in Women's Studies and their lives as monastics; the following are fine studies on medieval women monastics and spirituality. The following works would be recommended further reading: Judith M. Bennett, *Sisters and Workers in the Middle Ages* (Chicago: University of Chicago Press, 1989); Bruce L. Venarde, *Women's Monasticism and Medieval Society: Nunneries in France and England, 890–1215* (Ithaca, N.Y.: Cornell University Press, 1997). The pioneering study by Suzanne Fonay Wemple, *Women in Frankish Society: Marriage and the Cloister 500 to 900* (Philadelphia: University of Pennsylvania Press, 1981), surveys the general options of women in this early medieval period. Also recommended is the work on women spiritual writers by Emilie Zum Brunn and Georgette Epiney-Burgard, eds., *Women Mystics in Medieval Europe*, translated from the French by Sheila Hughes (New York: Paragon House, 1989). Penelope D. Johnson's *Equal in Monastic Profession: Religious Women in Medieval France* (Chicago: University of Chicago Press, 1991) is a wonderful analysis of the lives of women religious in context to their male counterparts. For a variety of issues and topics relating to women in the medieval monastic experience, one should consult the following excellent collection of essays:

John A. Nichols and Lillian Thomas Shank, eds., *Medieval Religious Women*, vols. 1–3 (Kalamazoo, Mich.: Cistercian Publications, 1984–95). For studies on particular women, the fine study by Barbara Newman, *Sister of Wisdom: St. Hildegard's Theology of the Feminine*, second edition (Berkeley: University of California Press, 1997), ought to be consulted, while spirituality and art receive treatment in Jeryldene Wood's *Women, Art, and Spirituality: The Poor Clares of Early Modern Italy* (Cambridge: Cambridge University Press, 1996).

ART AND ARCHITECTURE

In the fields of art and architecture, Walter William Horn and Ernest Born describe and provide detailed analysis of an early monastic monastery in their classic study *The Plan of St. Gall: A Study of the Architecture and Economy of and Life in a Paradigmatic Carolingian Monastery*, translation by Charles W. Jones of the Directives of Adalhard, 753–826, the Ninth Abbot of Corbie; and with a note by A. Hunter Dupree on the Significance of the Plan of St. Gall to the history of measurement (Berkeley: University of California Press, 1979). Two of the best treatments of the spirituality and rationale of the Cistercian order's aesthetic are: Terryl N. Kinder's *Cistercian Europe: Architecture of Contemplation* (Grand Rapids, Mich.: W. B. Eerdmans, 2002), and Conrad Rudolph, *The "Things of Greater Importance": Bernard of Clairvaux's Apologia and the Medieval Attitude Toward Art* (Philadelphia: University of Pennsylvania Press, 1990).

Medieval Institute Publications is a program
of The Medieval Institute, College of
Arts and Sciences, Western Michigan
University.

Typeset in 10/13 Caslon
Designed by Linda K. Judy
Composed by Julie Scrivener
at Medieval Institute Publications
Manufactured by Cushing-Malloy, Inc., Ann Arbor, Michigan

Medieval Institute Publications
College of Arts and Sciences
Western Michigan University
1903 W. Michigan Ave.
Kalamazoo, MI 49008-5432
www.wmich.edu/medieval

 WESTERN MICHIGAN UNIVERSITY